PANTONE

FOODMOOD

PANTONE
FOODMOOD

Guido Tommasi Editore

PANTONE®

Over fifty years ago Pantone revolutionized the graphic arts industry, launching the Pantone Matching System®, a standard that makes it possible for professionals working in graphic arts and publishing all over the world to delineate and faithfully reproduce colors. It is a universal language that, through the painstaking reproduction and classification of colors, has become a useful, precise, creative and thorough work tool. The Pantone color platform has been used in vastly different settings, and has reinforced its identity on one hand through the rigor of its design and the "golden rule" of proportions with which it is applied to licensed products; and on the other through the expressive strength of associated colors, their meanings and the emotions they arouse.

The Pantone Color Guides and Chips have become a permanent work tool, one that's always on hand: whether on a designer's desk or an art director's easel; in a craftsman's workshop or on a clothing designer's drawing table; in an architect's studio or a cosmetic creator's toolbox.

And in the kitchen? Is there a way to bring the Pantone philosophy to life on the stovetop? We found the idea of applying our guidelines in an environment frequented not only by professionals, but by a horde of aspiring "cooks and food designers," downright inspiring. That's how *Pantone Foodmood* was born… Enjoy!

Pantone Color Institute

FOODMOOD

The Pantone trademark is the very image of color, its physical version an irreplaceable work tool for architects, graphic artists and designers. Over time this modern, multiform synecdoche has become the very concept it represents.

Most languages use specific terms to indicate colors, but not all languages include the terminology necessary to describe the full range of universally-recognized colors: this depends on a given environment (the Eskimos, for example, use dozens of different definitions to describe different shades of white snow), cultural factors (in the past, many people didn't consider purple a color, but a shade of black), and the increasingly widespread trend of associating colors with important emotions.

This mechanism became that much more evident when we turned t square that o food, the essence of life and the privileged object of taste, as beautiful to behold as it is delicious or nourishing. Mankind has always sought to sublimate needs, and has turned the search for and preparation of food into an art form. The popular Italian proverb *si mangia prima con gli occhi che con la bocca* (the eyes eat before the mouth) lent credence to a simple fact: the eye always plays a part, deciding what's good by drinking in what's beautiful, even before taste can catapult us into the variegated universe of flavor.

On these pages, food encounters form and color in its clearest possible expression: Pantone. The little chip that has transformed color into a universal language has brought substance—food—to appear (and somehow also into being) in a new, different way, even as it continues to exist unaltered.

A new form of food… Has the educated palate been forced to submit to an enchantment of visual aesthetics? Will taste change, finding food in a new form?

Discover for yourself in this "chromatic cookbook": a potentially infinite, kaleidoscopic evolution; a heated dialogue between form and color and moods in which imagination and aesthetic sensibilities conquer and overwhelm the eyes.

Guido Tommasi

#colophon

_____

publisher
guido tommasi editore

art director and recipes design
francesca malerba

photographer
francesca moscheni

food stylist
livia sala

editorial project management
laura magda barazza

recipes
zino malerba

book design
buysschaert&malerba, milan
with sara travella

translations
anne ellis
with aaron maines (editing)

© guido tommasi editore, 2018
© buysschaert&malerba (recipes design)
ISBN 978 88 6753 208 7 – printed in Italy

THANKFULMOOD

What might have first appeared to be little more than an exercise in style—designing recipes according to the Pantone canon—proved to be a stimulating creative challenge. From the dinner table to the drawing table, the stovetop and ultimately the photo shoot, all those who participated in this project provided irreplaceable assistance, and the result of all their efforts was rendered at once edible and enjoyable in the dishes we're presenting on these pages.

Roberto Ruzzante launched the idea of putting Pantone on the table, paving the way for a series of entirely unique recipes to be created. Luca Trazzi, a designer par excellence, shared the philosophy and rigor of Pantone. The Pantone Color Institute ensured coherence throughout the project while Anne Ellis translated it.

Livia Sala, supported by Simone Liberati, built up the recipes with incredible expertise and precision; Francesca Moscheni—assisted by Laura Spinelli and Giampiero Lorenzi—provided the infallible eye necessary to capture the essence of each dish on film.

Laura Magda Barazza, who passionately followed the project every step of the way, left her "stamp" on every image and every page of this book.

Zino Malerba, an expert in cookbooks, reinterpreted classic recipes from all over the world with rigorous, Pantonian simplicity.

Sara Travella—Pantone Color Guides and Chips ever in hand—created the graphic design for the book and made the recipe drawings beautiful.

Last but not least, thanks go to Guido Tommasi, who had to wait a long time for the fruits of this labor and who, as an outstanding expert in all things gastronomical, inspired and faithfully followed our efforts to perfect *Pantone Foodmood*.

My heartfelt thanks to everyone!

Francesca Malerba

contents

recipes

The color of **sunshine**, **smiles**, promise, **enlightenment** and **hope**, yellow sparkles with **creativity**, **optimism** and **activity**. A wonderful color for **lifting the spirits**, yellow foods evoke **good cheer**.

yellow

rye bread appetizers

4 servings
preparation: 1 h + resting time
cooking: 10 min
difficulty: easy

---

12 slices whole grain rye bread

horseradish mousse
2 sheets of gelatin
120 g / 4 oz Greek yogurt
170 ml / 5 ½ fl oz drained sour
cream
60 g / 2 oz freshly grated
horseradish
45 ml / 1 ½ fl oz milk
100 ml / 3 ½ fl oz heavy cream
salt and pepper

hummus
200 g / 7 oz dried chickpeas
30 ml / 1 fl oz tahini
30 ml / 1 fl oz sesame oil
juice of 1 large organic lemon
Tabasco, to taste
1 garlic clove
salt

peanut butter
300 g / 10 oz shelled peanuts
50 g / 1 ¾ oz Demerara sugar
30 ml / 1 fl oz acacia honey
45 ml / 1 ½ fl oz peanut oil or
linseed oil

horseradish mousse
Soak the sheets of gelatin in cold water for 10 minutes.

Blend the yogurt, sour cream and grated horseradish.

Heat the milk in a small saucepan, add the drained gelatin and stir until dissolved.

Pour the gelatin and milk mixture into the yogurt mixture, gently combine and add salt to taste.

Whip the heavy cream and add it to the horseradish mixture, cover and refrigerate the mousse for at least 5 hours.

hummus
Cover and soak chickpeas in water for 8 hours. Boil until just tender. Drain, setting aside 200 ml / 6 ¾ fl oz of the cooking water.

Put them in a blender, add the tahini, sesame oil, lemon juice, a few drops of Tabasco and garlic, blend to create a creamy paste. Add salt to taste, blend, cover and refrigerate for 6 hours.

peanut butter
Toast peanuts on a baking sheet in the oven at 150 °C / 302 °F for 10 minutes. Transfer them to a dishtowel and rub gently to remove the skin, allow to cool.

Pour the peanuts into a food processor, add the sugar and honey and blend at low speed, adding peanut or linseed oil in a thin stream to obtain a smooth paste. Cover and refrigerate for at least 8 hours to set.

Cut the bread slices into 12 rectangles measuring approximately 5 x 10 cm / 2 x 4 in, spread 4 with horseradish mousse, 4 with hummus and 4 with peanut butter.

bumblebee polenta

4 servings
preparation: 1 h
cooking: 1 h
difficulty: medium

---

cod
500 g / 1 lb salt cod
200 ml / 6 ¾ fl oz milk
extra-virgin olive oil
chives, to taste
pink peppercorns, to taste
salt

polenta
400 g / 14 oz coarse yellow
cornmeal
400 g / 14 oz coarse white
cornmeal
1 or 2 squid ink packets
1 red pepper
1 green pepper
salt

cod
Soak the salt cod in a pan full of cold water. Add the milk and simmer gently, skimming the surface occasionally, until the cod is tender, about 20 minutes.

Drain, remove bones and transfer to a bowl, flake the flesh with a fork. Mix and add enough extra-virgin olive oil to create a creamy paste. Add salt if necessary. Add chopped chives and cracked pink peppercorns and set aside.

Lay peppers in a pan and roast in the oven at 180 °C / 356 °F for 20 minutes or until well browned. Remove from the oven, cover with a cloth until cooled, then remove the skin and cut into strips 1 cm / 0.40 in wide.

polenta
To prepare the yellow polenta, fill a pan with about 1 liter of lightly salted water. When it boils, sprinkle the cornmeal into the water while stirring constantly with a whisk to avoid lumping.

Cook for about 40 minutes; pour the polenta into a large rectangular mold brushed with water. Smooth the surface with a spatula, so the polenta is at least 2 cm / 0.80 in thick. Set aside to cool 10 minutes and cut into 4 rectangles measuring 8 x 11 cm / 3.15 x 4.40 in.

Prepare the black polenta according to the same procedure, using white cornmeal and adding squid ink after 10 minutes of cooking. When it has cooled a bit, cut into 8 rectangles measuring 4 x 6 cm / 1.60 x 2.40 in each.

Before serving, arrange a band of cod measuring 2 cm / 0.80-in on each piece of yellow polenta, and a 1-cm / 0.40-in strip of red or green pepper on each piece of black polenta.

risotto with parmigiano tuiles

4 servings
preparation: 30 min
cooking: 30 min
difficulty: medium

parmigiano tuiles
250 g / 8 oz grated Parmigiano
Reggiano cheese

risotto
320 g / 11 ¼ oz Carnaroli rice
80 g / 3 oz butter
50 g / 1 ¾ oz grated
Parmigiano Reggiano cheese
30 g / 1 oz beef bone marrow
1 white onion
200 ml / 6 ¾ fl oz white wine
1 l mild beef broth
2 saffron powder sachets
salt and black peppercorns

parmigiano tuiles
Distribute the Parmigiano evenly in a pan lined with cooking paper, and bake in an oven at 200 °C / 392 °F until the surface begins to bubble and becomes lightly golden. Allow it to harden slightly, then slide it onto a cutting board and cut it into a 8.5 x 11 cm / 3.35 x 4.40 in rectangle. Prepare 3 more Parmigiano tuiles and set them aside.

risotto
To prepare the risotto, mince the onion and cook gently in a pot over low heat with 50 g / 1 ¾ oz of butter and the beef bone marrow.

When the onion is transparent, add the rice and toast it for a few minutes or until the grains are translucent.

Add the wine and reduce, then add 2 ladles of boiling broth and cook the rice at a simmer, adding more boiling broth only when the previous ladleful has been absorbed.

In the meantime, soak the saffron in a little hot broth for about 5 minutes. When the risotto is almost ready, add the saffron, continue to stir and finish cooking. Add salt to taste, add the rest of the butter and 50 g / 1 ¾ oz of Parmigiano. Cover and allow risotto to rest for 5 minutes.

Place a square 6 x 6 cm / 2.40 x 2.40 in pastry cutter on each Parmigiano tuile and fill it with 2 cm / 0.80 in of risotto. Garnish with freshly crushed black peppercorns and serve immediately.

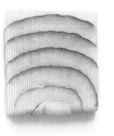

truffled quail eggs

4 servings
preparation: 20 min + resting time
cooking: 5 min
difficulty: easy

12 quail eggs
12 slices whole grain rye
bread
butter

flavored butter
400 g / 14 oz butter
1 small white truffle
1 bunch fresh chives

Soften the butter at room temperature.

In the meantime, clean the truffle using a damp paper towel or a brush and then dry. Rinse and dry the chives then mince.

Put the softened butter into 2 bowls and cream it with a wooden spoon or whisk. Grate the truffle into one bowl, and the chives into the other. Blend to achieve a homogeneous cream.

Transfer the creamed butter mixtures onto 2 pieces of plastic wrap, mold into rectangular cakes 5 x 1.5 cm / 2 x 0.60 in and transfer to the refrigerator for 2 hours.

Cut the bread into 12 rectangular slices measuring 4.5 x 6.5 cm / 1.80 x 2.60 in.

Fry the quail eggs sunny side up in a small pan with a small amount of unflavored butter. When the whites are cooked, transfer them to a cutting board.

Cut the eggs with a lightly oiled pastry cutter to make squares measuring 3.5 x 3.5 cm / 1.40 x 1.40 in. Arrange each egg on a rectangle of rye bread and cut out the blocks of butter into 12 rectangles measuring 4.5 x 1.5 cm / 1.80 x 0.60 in. Accompany each tartine with one rectangle of each type of flavored butter.

lemon linguine

4 servings
preparation: 15 min
cooking: 10 min
difficulty: easy

---

280 g / 10 oz linguine
2 small organic lemons
75 g / 3 oz butter
30 ml / 1 fl oz olive oil
200 ml / 6 ¾ fl oz heavy cream
grated Parmigiano Reggiano
cheese, to taste
salt and black peppercorns

Melt the butter in a pan, add the olive oil and the grated lemon zest.

Warm the mixture in the pan over low heat for 5 minutes, then add the cream, mix and heat. Do not allow the sauce to boil. Salt to taste.

Cook the linguine in plenty of salted water, drain when *al dente* and dress with the lemon sauce.

Arrange on dinner plates and serve with a dusting of Parmigiano and coarsely crushed black peppercorns.

PANTONE
UNIVERSE™
18-3224 TPX C

deconstructed russian salad

4 servings
preparation: 15 min
cooking: 15 min
difficulty: easy

---

8 eggs

mayonnaise
2 egg yolks
juice of 1 organic lemon
200 ml / 6 ¾ fl oz vegetable oil
salt and pepper

topping
3 baby carrots
100 g / 3 ½ oz fresh garden peas
100 g / 3 ½ oz fresh corn kernels

Prepare the mayonnaise in a tall narrow container like a jar or a large glass, with egg yolks at room temperature. Add salt and pepper and whip the yolks by hand.

Add the vegetable oil in a thin steady stream and a few drops of lemon juice. Continue whisking while alternating the ingredients until the sauce has a dense consistency. To prevent the mayonnaise from curdling, always whisk in the same direction and pour the oil very slowly.

Steam the vegetables until *al dente*, then remove them from the heat to cool.

Cut the carrots into circles.

Hard boil the eggs, cool and cut them in half lengthwise, remove the yolks with a teaspoon.

Fill the eggs with the mayonnaise, smoothing the surface and garnishing with the vegetables.

mango pudding with panna cotta

4 servings
preparation: 40 min + resting time
cooking: 10 min
difficulty: challenging

mango pudding
500 g / 1 lb mango flesh
150 g / 5 oz Demerara sugar
4 ½ sheets of gelatin
granulated sugar

panna cotta
250 ml / 8 fl oz heavy cream
50 ml / 1 ¾ fl oz milk
90 g / 3 oz sugar
2 sheets of gelatin

mango pudding
To prepare the mango pudding, soak the sheets of gelatin in cold water for 20 minutes. In the meantime, dissolve the sugar in 200 ml / 6 ¾ fl oz of water and cook over low heat to obtain a syrup. Squeeze excess water from the gelatin, add the gelatin to the syrup and mix until it is dissolved. Allow to cool until the gelatin begins to congeal.

Mix the mango in a blender, strain and add it to the preparation, stirring to create a homogeneous mixture.

Fill 4 round molds measuring 8.5 cm / 3.35 in in diameter with the mixture, ensuring the pudding mix is 4 cm / 1.60 in deep. Cover and refrigerate for 6 hours to set.

When the pudding has set, prepare the panna cotta.

panna cotta
Soak the sheets of gelatin in cold water for 20 minutes.

Pour the cream and the milk into a small saucepan, add sugar and scald. Remove from heat before it boils. Squeeze excess water from the sheets of gelatin then add them to the cream and continue to cook until gelatin is completely dissolved. Set aside to cool a little.

Using a round pastry cutter measuring 3.5 cm / 1.40 in in diameter, cut a hole in the center of each mango pudding, then cut a 1.5 cm / 0.60 in-wide band to the edge of the mold.

Pour the panna cotta into a pastry bag and fill in the mango pudding. Cover and place in the refrigerator for at least 6 hours.

Remove the pudding from the refrigerator ten minutes before serving, turn the individual servings onto plates and sprinkle the top with granulated sugar.

tarte citron

4 servings
preparation: 30 min + resting time
cooking: 30 min
difficulty: challenging

---

shortcrust pastry
1 organic lemon
130 g / 4 ½ oz salted butter
100 g / 3 ½ oz sugar
1 egg
200 g / 7 oz all-purpose flour
50 g / 1 ¾ oz rice flour
dried legumes (beans or
chickpeas etc.) or ceramic pie
weights

lemon filling
2 large juicy organic lemons
100 g / 3 ½ oz butter
100 g / 3 ½ oz sugar
3 eggs

meringues
2 egg whites
50 g / 1 ¾ oz granulated sugar
50 g / 1 ¾ oz confectioner's
sugar
½ tsp organic lemon juice
salt

shortcrust pastry
Grate the lemon zest into a bowl. Cut the softened butter into small pieces and add them to the bowl with the sugar. Work the mixture for 15 minutes to obtain an airy, creamy mixture.

Incorporate the egg and sifted flour. Continue to work, blending with fingertips to produce a smooth dough. Gather the dough into a ball and cover in plastic wrap. Allow to rest in the refrigerator for at least an hour.

Roll out the dough in a thin layer. Line a square mold measuring 15 cm x 15 cm / 5.90 x 5.90 in, prick the dough with a fork, cover with cooking paper and weigh it down with dried legumes. Bake for 10 minutes at 180 °C / 356 °F. Remove the paper and legumes and continue to cook for 20 minutes. Cool on a rack.

lemon filling
Wash the lemons and grate the zest. Juice the lemons and add the juice of the one used to prepare the shortbread. You will need 225 ml / 8 fl oz. Juice another lemon if necessary.

Melt the butter in a double boiler, add the sugar and stir until dissolved. Beat the eggs separately. Add the eggs, lemon zest and lemon juice to the butter and sugar mixture, stirring continuously. Continue to cook to produce a smooth cream. Cover, allow to cool at room temperature and then place in the refrigerator.

Fill the tart with the lemon cream. Smooth the surface and cover with plastic wrap. Allow it to set in the refrigerator for 2 hours.

Just before serving, garnish 1/3 of the lemon cream with the meringues you prepared following the recipe on page 92.

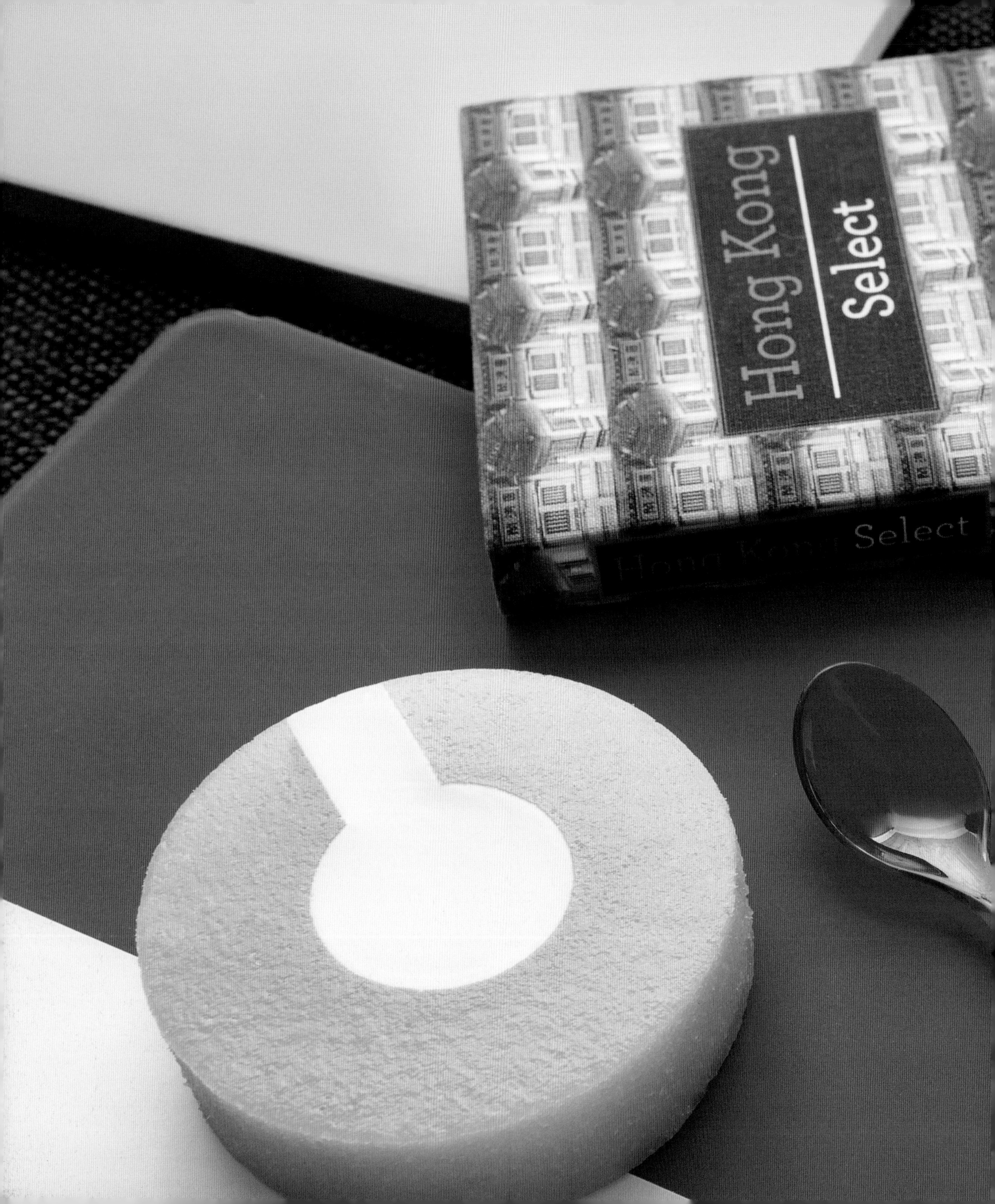
Hong Kong
Select

Fun-loving and **energetic**, orange is a known **appetite stimulant**. **Vibrant** and **warm**, orange lovers are **good natured**, expansive, **extroverted** with a disposition as **bright** as their favorite color.

orange

gazpacho

4 servings
preparation: 20 min + resting time
no cooking
difficulty: easy

---

1 kg / 2 lb ripe tomatoes
1 cucumber
100 g / 3 ½ oz red onion
1 sweet green pepper
1 garlic clove
150 g / 5 oz stale crusty white bread
50 ml / 1 ¾ fl oz extra-virgin olive oil
30 ml / 1 fl oz white wine vinegar
salt

Scald the tomatoes for a few seconds in boiling water, run cold water over them, peel and cut into quarters. Remove the seeds.

Peel the cucumber and onion, remove seeds and membranes from the peppers, dice all the vegetables and put in a bowl with the peeled and lightly crushed garlic. Stir together.

Soften the bread in water, squeezing to make sure any excess water is removed. Put all ingredients in a food processor and mix until the mixture is smooth.

Add extra-virgin olive oil and vinegar, salt to taste and blend well.

Pour into a soup tureen, cover and refrigerate for 3 hours prior to serving.

cheddar with aromatic jams

4 servings
preparation: 1 h + resting time
cooking: 2 h
difficulty: easy

---

250 g / 8 oz cheddar

mango chutney
1 mango
200 g / 7 oz Demerara sugar
10 g / ½ oz curcuma
½ tsp cinnamon powder
1 ½ tsp cocoa nibs
20 g / ¾ oz fresh ginger
½ chili pepper
1 shallot
200 ml / 6 ¾ fl oz apple cider vinegar
salt

fig jam
500 g / 1 lb figs
1 large organic lemon
400 g / 14 oz Demerara sugar

red onion marmalade
500 g / 1 lb Tropea red onions
300 g / 10 oz Demerara sugar
1 bay leaf
slivered almonds, to taste
100 ml / 3 ½ fl oz white wine

mango chutney
Peel the mango and remove the seed, cut the fruit into cubes and put them in a small, heavy-bottomed saucepan. Add the sugar, curcuma, cinnamon, crushed cocoa nibs and grated ginger. Stir and set aside for 3 hours.

Add the chili pepper, shallots and vinegar. Salt to taste and cook the chutney over very low heat for 2 hours, stirring occasionally. Allow to cool.

fig jam
Peel the figs and cut into 4. Zest the lemon, making narrow strips, juice the lemon into a pan and add the figs and zest.

Cook, stirring continuously, for about 10 minutes, then add the sugar and continue to cook for about 45 minutes, skimming the surface occasionally. If the jam remains too liquid, add more sugar and continue to cook until you achieve the desired density. Allow to cool.

red onion marmalade
Peel the onions and cut them into thin slices with a mandoline slicer. Transfer them into a pan, pour in the sugar, add the bay leaf, slivered almonds, wine and mix.

Cover and allow the marmalade to rest in a cool place for 8 hours. Remove the bay leaf and cook for 40 minutes or until it is compact. Allow to cool.

Cut the cheddar into 12 rectangles measuring 4.5 x 6 cm / 1.80 x 2.40 in each, distribute the jams and serve.

frittata with radicchio & walnut salad

4 servings
preparation: 10 min
cooking: 10 min
difficulty: easy

---

salad
1 large head of radicchio
1 blood orange
1 pink grapefruit
20 chopped walnuts
Parmigiano Reggiano flakes
extra-virgin olive oil
salt and pepper

frittata
8 eggs
100 g / 3 ½ oz grated
Parmigiano Reggiano cheese
extra-virgin olive oil
salt and pepper

salad
Wash the radicchio and cut it into strips, peel the orange and grapefruit with a sharp knife, removing the membrane and cutting into cubes. Add walnuts and dress with extra-virgin olive oil. Salt and pepper to taste. Set aside in a cool place.

frittata
Break the eggs into a large bowl, add the grated Parmigiano, add salt and pepper, and mix with a fork or whisk.

Oil a large square pan with a little olive oil; pour the eggs in and tilt the pan to distribute the mixture evenly.

Place in the oven and cook at 200 °C / 392 °F for 10 minutes until the frittata puffs up and is golden brown.

Allow to cool for 5 minutes, turn the frittata out onto a cutting board and cut into 4 rectangles measuring 11 x 15 cm / 4.40 x 5.90 in each. Set aside to cool.

Place on the frittata a square cookie cutter measuring 8 x 8 cm / 3.15 x 3.15 in, fill it with 2 or 3 tablespoons of salad and remove carefully. Do the same with the other pieces of frittata. Garnish with Parmigiano flakes and serve.

red mullet on sweet potato

4 servings
preparation: 30 min
cooking: 15 min
difficulty: medium

2 sweet potatoes
20 red mullet fillet
butter
extra-virgin olive oil, to taste
1 organic lemon
salt
pink peppercorns

Slice the potatoes into disks and arrange them on a cookie sheet covered with baking paper; brush them with a little olive oil and cook at 180 °C / 356 °F for 15 minutes.

Using tweezers, remove any remaining bones from the fish fillets. Rinse them under water and dry with a paper towel.

Melt the butter in a small saucepan over low heat.

Brush the 4 fillets with the melted butter, then cook them in a nonstick pan for 5 minutes, turning once.

Place them on a paper towel to absorb excess oil, add salt to taste and keep warm.

Remove the flesh from the remaining fillets and cut it into cubes.

Heat a little extra-virgin olive oil in a nonstick pan, add the cubed fish, season with a tablespoon of grated lemon zest and cook for 3 minutes.

Arrange the potatoes in a single layer on baking paper, over-lapping them slightly. Using a sharp knife, cut 4 rectangles measuring 10 x 12 cm / 4 x 4.70 each, then carefully transfer them onto 4 plates using a wide spatula.

Place one fillet and 1/4 of the red mullet cubes on the square of potatoes, then drizzle with extra-virgin olive oil and dust with crushed pink peppercorns.

carrot salad with kefta

4 servings
preparation: 30 min + resting time
cooking: 20 min
difficulty: medium

unleavened spelt flatbread

salad
3 carrots
juice of 1 organic lemon
raw unshelled pumpkin and
sunflower seeds
1 bunch parsley
extra-virgin olive oil
salt

yogurt and mint sauce
100 g / 3 ½ oz Greek yogurt
mint, to taste
extra-virgin olive oil
½ garlic clove

kefta
250 g / 8 oz ground beef
120 g / 4 oz stale bread
white wine vinegar
1 tsp chopped mint leaves
1 tsp chopped parsley
1 small golden onion
2 eggs
1 zucchini
paprika
cumin and cinnamon powder
extra-virgin olive oil
salt and pepper

salad
Peel the carrots and cut into narrow strips using a vegetable peeler. Put the strips in a large bowl, add a few drops of lemon juice, the pumpkin and sunflower seeds and chopped parsley. Dress with a little olive oil, cover and set aside in the refrigerator.

yogurt and mint sauce
Pour the yogurt into a bowl, add the mint and chopped garlic and a small drizzle of oil, then blend well. Allow the sauce to rest for at least 1 hour before serving.

kefta
Break the stale bread into small pieces in a bowl, wet it with a little white vinegar and set aside.

Place the meat in a bowl, squeeze the excess vinegar from the bread and add it, together with the eggs, onion, chopped parsley and mint, plus a pinch each of paprika, cumin and cinnamon. Add salt and pepper to taste. Work the ingredients together well to obtain a soft but stiff paste, cover and refrigerate for 2 hours.

Lightly oil a 3-cm / 1.20-in square pastry cutter and fill with the meat mixture to create 8 small loaves at least 3 cm / 1.20 in high each. Cook the kefta in a nonstick pan with a little extra-virgin olive oil until they are golden brown.

Slice the zucchini to make disks and grill. Take 4 wooden skewers and alternate 2 kefta and one zucchini disk.

Cut the unleavened flatbread into 4 rectangles measuring 12 x 15 cm / 4.70 x 5.90 in each, garnish with the salad using a square pastry form measuring 10 x 10 cm / 4 x 4 in and tweezers.

fruit salad and sesame brittle

4 servings
preparation: 40 min
cooking: 10 min
difficulty: medium

---

brittle
300 g / 10 oz sesame seeds
50 g / 1 ¾ oz flax seeds
200 g / 7 oz sugar
1 pinch of vanillin

fruit salad
grapes
peaches
apples
juice of 1 small organic lemon
Demerara sugar, to taste

brittle
Put the seeds in a pan covered with baking paper and toast in the oven at 180 °C / 356 °F for a few minutes, being careful not to scorch them.

Put the sugar in a nonstick pan, add 2 or 3 tablespoons of water and heat until it caramelizes.

Add the seeds (except for one spoonful) while they are still hot and flavor with a pinch of vanillin.

Pour the mixture on a marble slab and work it with 2 spatulas to make a homogeneous mass.

Spread the seed mass on a baking sheet lined with baking paper and set aside to cool slightly. While the seed mass is still warm, use a kitchen knife to make 4 bases measuring 11 x 15 cm / 4.40 x 5.90 in each.

fruit salad
Cut fruit into small pieces and transfer to a bowl. Squeeze a few drops of lemon juice over the fruit pieces and add some sugar.

Distribute the fruit salad on the pieces of brittle in squares measuring 8.5 x 8.5 cm / 3.35 x 3.35 in each, using a pastry cutter to shape the arrangement and serve.

The color of **hearth** and **home**, brown represents **roots** and a steady, **stable** source of **security** and **comfort**. Swinging from wholesome and **organic** to **enticingly delectable** and decadent, it is always a staple presence and **persistent persuader** in the kitchen.

brown

chicken teriyaki with black beans

4 servings
preparation: 1 h + resting time
cooking: 2 h
difficulty: medium

chicken teriyaki
320 g / 11 ¼ oz chicken breast
extra-virgin olive oil
chives
125 ml / 4 fl oz soy sauce
30 ml / 1 fl oz mirin
15 ml / ½ fl oz sugar

bean salad
100 g / 3 ½ oz dried black
beans
½ carrot
½ shallot
1 tsp cumin seed
½ golden onion
extra-virgin olive oil
salt

bean salad
Soak the beans in cold water for 8 hours. Drain and transfer into a pan full of lightly salted water, add the carrot and shallot and cook for 1 hour and 30 minutes.

Drain the beans, transfer them into a bowl and cool. Season with extra-virgin olive oil, cumin seeds and diced onion. Add salt to taste and refrigerate.

chicken teriyaki
Pour the soy sauce, mirin and sugar into a small, heavy-bottomed saucepan. Cook over low heat, stirring until the sugar is dissolved.

Raise the heat and bring to a boil. Allow to simmer for 5 minutes. Remove from heat and set aside.

Pound the chicken breast and eliminate any cartilage, bones or fat. Cut into cubes.

Heat a little oil in a frying pan or wok, add the chicken and sauté until golden. Pour the teriyaki sauce over it. Cover and cook for 30 minutes.

Place a 14-cm / 5.50-in round pastry cutter on a plate; fill the upper half with chicken and the lower half with beans. Delicately remove the pastry cutter and arrange the other portions.

Sprinkle chopped chives over the chicken and serve.

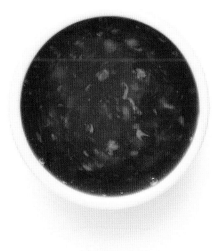

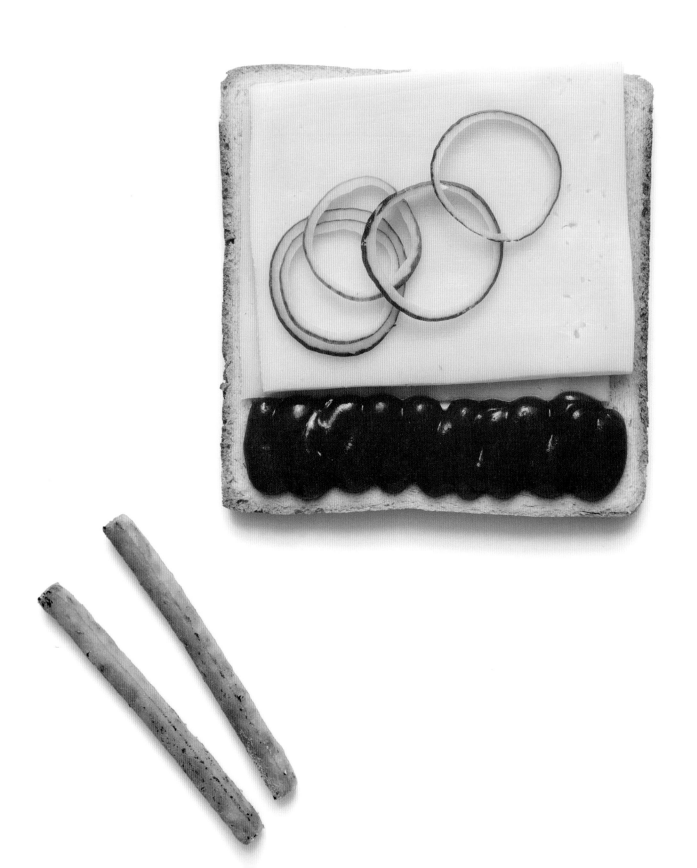

square burger with french fries

4 servings
preparation: 40 min
cooking: 20 min
difficulty: medium

---

1 loaf of white sandwich bread
1 head of iceberg lettuce
1 red onion
8 Edam or cheddar cheese
slices

burger
800 g / 1 ¾ lb ground chuck
olive oil
coarse sea salt
salt and pepper

french fries
800 g / 1 ¾ lb potatoes
sunflower oil
salt

mustard
ketchup

Cut the bread into 8 square slices measuring 12 x 12 cm / 4.70 x 4.70 in and at least 2 cm / 0.80 in thick, then slice the onion crosswise into rings. Wash the lettuce and dry carefully. Set aside.

burger
Put the meat in a large bowl, add salt and pepper to taste and break it apart. Divide it into 4 portions. Place them on a cutting board and shape the burgers using a lightly oiled pastry cutter measuring 12 x 7 cm / 4.70 x 2.80 in. Set aside to rest for 1 hour.

Heat a grill pan, sprinkle some coarse salt and place the burgers on it. Cook the meat until it comes away from the pan by itself, turn it and continue cooking on the other side. Never press the burgers because they will lose their cooking juices, leaving the meat dry.

french fries
While the burgers are resting, wash the potatoes, dry them, peel and cut them into sticks. Soak the sticks in very cold water for 5 minutes, then put them in another bowl of hot water and soak for 10 minutes. Drain and pat dry carefully.

Just before you are ready to grill the burgers, pour cooking sunflower oil into a frying pan. When the sunflower oil is hot add the potatoes and fry, turning them occasionally. When they are golden, place them on a paper towel and salt to taste.

Take a slice of bread, place a piece of lettuce on it, a burger and arrange the mustard using a pastry bag with a medium tip. Next take another slice of bread, place the cheese cut to size, a few rings of onion and add ketchup to taste. Serve the hamburger open-faced to show the ingredients

Serve with French fries.

round vegetarian burger

4 servings
preparation: 40 min + resting time
cooking: 1 h and 30 min
difficulty: easy

150 g / 5 oz dried lentils
150 g / 5 oz dried chickpeas
4 carrots
2 shallots
1 tsp cumin powder
1 garlic clove
1 potato
corn flour
breadcrumbs
extra-virgin olive oil
salt and pepper
sweet mustard

Soak the lentils in cold water for 8 hours, drain and transfer into a pot with lightly salted water. Add 2 carrots and one shallot and cook for 1 hour. Prepare the chickpeas the same way.

Drain the lentils with a skimmer and set aside to cool.

Cut the potato into cubes, then cook in plenty of oil. Drain and salt to taste.

Heat some oil in a nonstick pan, add the garlic and cook until it is just golden. Remove the garlic and add the lentils and chickpeas. Sprinkle with cumin. Add salt and pepper and cook for 10 minutes or until the legumes are dry.

Put the legumes in a food processor and blend until they have become a homogeneous paste, then transfer the paste to a bowl, add the potatoes and enough breadcrumbs to make a dense mixture.

Make 4 round patties out of the mixture measuring 12 cm / 4.70 in in diameter. Turn the patties in the corn flour and place them on a baking sheet lined with cooking paper.

Bake in the oven at 180 °C / 356 °F for 20 minutes, turning once after 10 minutes.

Serve with sweet mustard.

pissaladière

4 servings
preparation: 30 min
cooking: 1 h
difficulty: easy

---

500 g / 1 lb bread dough
500 g / 1 lb white onions
1 garlic clove
120 g / 4 oz salted anchovy
fillets in olive oil
100 g / 3 ½ oz black olives
oregano
6 red new potatoes
extra-virgin olive oil
salt and pepper

Heat some oil in a pan, add the thinly sliced onion and finely chopped garlic; cook until soft for 10 minutes, stirring continuously.

Season with salt and pepper, cover and continue to cook for 40 minutes, stirring from time to time and making sure the onions do not brown.

Clean the salt off the anchovies by rinsing them under running water, then pat dry with a paper towel.

Wash the potatoes and cut them into slices without peeling them. Scald them for 2 minutes in boiling water, drain and set aside.

Roll out the dough and divide it into 4 rectangles measuring 12 x 13 cm / 4.70 x 5.10 in each. Pinch up the edges to make a frame, then transfer them onto a lightly oiled baking sheet.

Arrange the onions, anchovies and olives on the pissaladière and drizzle with oil. At the bottom, arrange a row of potatoes and dust with oregano.

Bake the pissaladière in a preheated oven at 180 °C / 356 °F for 30 minutes, remove from the oven and serve.

coffee semifreddo

4 servings
preparation: 15 min + resting time
no cooking
difficulty: easy

---

semifreddo
6 egg yolks
180 g / 6 oz sugar
180 ml / 6 fl oz freshly-made
cold coffee
15 ml / ½ fl oz instant coffee
600 ml / 20 fl oz heavy cream

decoration
coffee beans or chocolate-
covered coffee beans
white chocolate drops or
chips

Put the egg yolks and sugar in a bowl and beat them with an electric beater until they are light and foamy, then add the coffee while continuing to stir.

Add the instant coffee and pour the mixture into a small, heavy-bottomed saucepan. Cook over low heat while stirring continuously until the cream coats the spoon.

Allow to cool. Delicately fold in the whipped cream lifting the mixture up from the bottom to incorporate it without losing the mixture's airy consistency.

Pour the mixture into a rectangular pan to create a layer at least 1 cm / 0.40 in thick, level the surface, cover and leave in the freezer for at least 6 hours.

Cut the semifreddo into 4 rectangles measuring 9 x 13 cm / 3.5 x 5.10 in each. Using tweezers, decorate them with coffee beans and white chocolate drops.

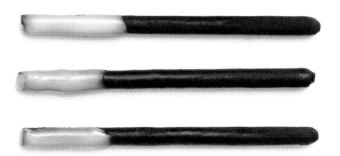

brownies&whities

4 servings
preparation: 30 min
cooking: 40 min
difficulty: easy

---

dark chocolate brownies
150 g / 5 oz butter
200 g / 7 oz sugar
180 g / 6 oz dark chocolate
½ tsp vanilla extract
2 eggs
60 g / 2 oz all-purpose flour
20 g / ¾ oz dark cocoa powder
100 g / 3 ½ oz pecans
salt

white chocolate brownies
150 g / 5 oz butter
200 g / 7 oz sugar
180 g / 6 oz white chocolate
½ tsp vanilla extract
2 eggs
60 g / 2 oz all-purpose flour

decoration
dark chocolate cubes
candied orange zest

To prepare the dark chocolate brownies, break the chocolate into small pieces and cut the butter into cubes. Put both ingredients in a double boiler. Add sugar, a pinch of salt and melt together while stirring so that the butter and chocolate form a smooth cream.

Cool slightly, add the vanilla and beat in the eggs, one at a time, stirring continuously.

Sift the flour and cocoa powder directly into the chocolate cream. Stir energetically for 10 minutes.

Add the chopped pecans and blend into the mixture with a spatula.

Pour batter into a rectangular pan lined with baking paper to create a layer at least 2 cm / 0.80 in thick, level the surface and bake in the oven for 20 minutes. When ready, transfer to a cooling rack and allow to cool slightly.

While the dark chocolate brownies are cooking, prepare the white chocolate ones the same way.

Cut the brownies into rectangles measuring 5 x 6.5 cm / 2 x 2.60 in each. Use a pastry cutter or long tweezers to decorate the brownies by forming a square roughly measuring 3 cm / 1.20 in on each with small chocolate cubes and candied orange zest.

tiramisù

4 servings
preparation: 15 min + resting time
no cooking
difficulty: easy

---

3 eggs
60 g / 2 oz sugar
250 g / 8 oz mascarpone
freshly-made cold coffee,
to taste
250 g / 8 oz savoiardi or
ladyfingers
camporelli cookies with pearl
sugar or pavesini
dark cocoa powder, to taste

Put the egg yolks and sugar in a bowl and beat them with an electric beater until they are light and foamy, then gradually add the mascarpone and continue to mix until it is a homogeneous cream.

Beat the egg whites until they are stiff and fold them into the cream, lifting the mixture up from the bottom to incorporate it without losing its airy consistency.

Line a rectangular disposable aluminum baking pan with baking paper so that it hangs over on 2 edges. Create a layer of lady fingers, brush the biscuits with a little coffee, pour some of the mascarpone cream over it. Repeat with another layer of biscuits, coffee and mascarpone cream.

Smooth the surface and cover with plastic wrap. Leave in the refrigerator for 3 hours.

Cut the corners of the pan, being careful not to ruin the dessert, pull the baking paper in order to move it and transfer it with a cake lifter directly onto a serving dish.

Cut a 3 cm / 1.20 in-high rectangular band from a piece of cardboard. Place the band 3 cm / 1.20 in from the bottom and sprinkle cocoa powder through a sieve over the rest of the tiramisù.

Carefully remove the cardboard, arrange cookies around the tiramisù and serve.

moist chocolate cake

4 servings
preparation: 20 min
cooking: 30 min
difficulty: easy

---

250 g / 8 oz dark chocolate
50 ml / 1 ¾ fl oz milk
250 g / 8 oz melted butter
6 eggs
100 g / 3 ½ oz all-purpose flour
250 g / 8 oz sugar
100 g / 3 ½ oz ground almonds

decoration
colored sugar crystals
confectioner's sugar

Break the chocolate into a double boiler, add the milk and heat over very low heat to melt the chocolate.

Add the melted butter and work with a whisk to blend it into the chocolate.

Add one egg yolk at a time and stir until completely mixed in before adding the next.

Pour in the sifted flour while stirring continuously to prevent lumping, add the sugar and the almonds.

Remove from the heat and continue to work the mixture for 5 more minutes. Allow to cool.

Beat the egg whites to form stiff peaks and fold them into the chocolate carefully, lifting the mixture up from the bottom to incorporate it without losing the airy consistency.

Pour the mixture into a buttered and floured cake pan measuring 15 x 20 cm / 6 x 7.90 in, and bake at 160 °C / 320 °F for 30 minutes. Allow to cool.

Create two cardboard stencils, one measuring 3 x 11 cm / 1.20 x 4.40 in, the other measuring 11 x 11 cm / 4.40 x 4.40 in. Place them over the cake, leaving 2.5 cm / 1 in from the top and 2.5 cm / 1 in from the bottom. Decorate with colored sugar crystals and confectioner's sugar. Carefully remove the stencil and serve.

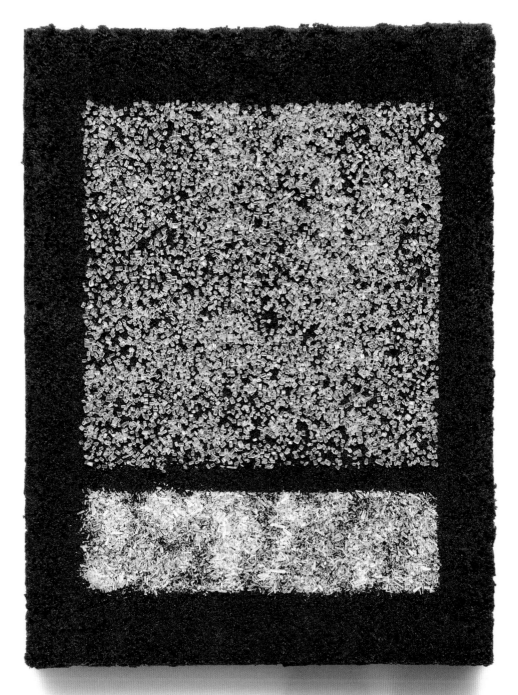

Bold and **vibrant**, red is the color of **life** itself. An enticing shade with mouthwatering appeal, red is the color family of a wide variety of **luscious** and **nourishing** foods that sustain our very existence.

red

tomato aspic

6 servings
preparation: 45 min + resting time
cooking: 20 min
difficulty: medium

---

pâte brisée
300 g / 10 oz all-purpose flour
150 g / 5 oz salted butter
30 ml / 1 fl oz oregano

aspic
500 ml / 16 fl oz tomato juice
10 g / ½ oz sheets of gelatin
15 ml / ½ fl oz chopped chives
15 ml / ½ fl oz Demerara sugar
15 ml / ½ fl oz organic lemon juice

cheese cream
100 g / 3 ½ oz cream cheese
50 g / 1 ¾ oz Greek yogurt
1 bunch chives

pâte brisée
Sift the flour into a mound with a well in the center, put the softened butter and oregano in the middle. Blend together using fingertips to make a lumpy dough.

Form a new well, pour 8 tablespoons of ice cold water in the center and blend just enough to create a homogeneous ball of dough. Wrap it in plastic wrap and set aside to rest for 2 hours in the least cold section of the refrigerator.

aspic
Pour the tomato juice into a pan, add the chopped chives, sugar and cook over low heat for 15 minutes without boiling.

Soak the sheets of gelatin in cold water for 20 minutes. Squeeze to remove any excess water then add the gelatin to the tomato mixture and stir until fully dissolved. Add lemon juice and strain the preparation into a rectangular nonstick pan. The liquid should fill it to 1 cm / 0.40 in. Cover and refrigerate for 6 hours, then cut rectangles measuring 4.5 x 6 cm / 1.80 x 2.40 in.

Preheat oven to 180 °C / 356 °F. Roll out the refrigerated dough and place it on a baking sheet lined with baking paper. Prick the surface with a fork and bake for 20 minutes. Remove it from the pan and allow to cool slightly, then cut into rectangles measuring 4.5 x 6 cm / 1.80 x 2.40 in.

cheese cream
Combine the cheese and yogurt at room temperature. Add the finely chopped chives and blend to a soft, smooth consistency.

Arrange the aspic rectangles on the pâte brisée, then garnish with the cheese spread using a square pastry cutter measuring 3 cm / 1.20 in.

terrines

4 servings
preparation: 30 min
no cooking
difficulty: easy

white sandwich bread
1 jar red lumpfish roe
butter

taramosalata
220 g / 8 oz stale white bread
150 g / 5 oz taramas (carp roe)
15 ml / ½ fl oz chopped golden
onion
juice of 1 organic lemon
100 ml / 3 ½ fl oz extra-virgin
olive oil

guacamole
2 avocados
1 spring onion
1 ripe tomato
juice of 1 organic lemon
Tabasco
salt

taramosalata

Cut the crust off the bread, break it into pieces and put it in a bowl, then allow it to soften in a little lukewarm water for 5 minutes. Squeeze out excess water.

Place the taramas, onion, lemon juice and a little extra-virgin olive oil in the bowl of a food processor to form a paste.

Add the bread and process, adding the remaining olive oil in a thin stream until the mixture becomes a smooth cream.

Cover and set aside to cool in the refrigerator.

guacamole

Eliminate the green parts of the spring onion and mince. Cut the tomato in half, remove seeds and cut into cubes.

Cut the avocados in half. Remove the pit and scrape the flesh out into a bowl with a spoon. Pour lemon juice over it and add a drop of Tabasco; then mash with a fork to create a creamy mixture.

Add the tomato and onion, stirring gently. Cover the guacamole and leave in the refrigerator. Add salt to taste before serving.

Cut the bread into 12 rectangular slices measuring 4 x 5.5 cm / 1.60 x 2.20 in. Spread 4 slices with the softened butter, making squares measuring 3 x 3 cm / 1.20 x 1.20 in. Cover with the lumpfish eggs. Then garnish 4 slices with the taramosalata and the remaining 4 with guacamole.

square pizza

4 servings
preparation: 30 min + resting time
cooking: 15 min
difficulty: medium

---

350 g / 12 oz 00 flour (highly refined flour)
150 g / 5 oz manitoba flour (extra strong bread flour: W 360–450)
7 g / ¼ oz active dry yeast powder
1 tsp granulated sugar
50 ml / 1 ¾ fl oz extra-virgin olive oil
15 g / ½ oz salt

150 g / 5 oz Pachino tomatoes
150 g / 5 oz yellow cherry tomatoes
bocconcini (mini mozzarella balls)
fresh basil leaves, to taste
black peppercorns

Temper the yeast and sugar in 50 ml / 1 ¾ fl oz of lukewarm water and set aside for 15 minutes.

Sift the 2 kinds of flour together directly into a stand mixer, turn it on and add 300 milliliters of water at room temperature in a thin stream, mixing with a dough hook on the slowest speed.

While the dough is being kneaded, add the dissolved yeast in a thin stream, salt and continue to knead until the dough is solid and comes away from the sides of the bowl. Gradually pour in the extra-virgin olive oil and continue to knead until it has been completely absorbed.

Turn the oven on to the lowest setting for just a few minutes, then turn it off. Remove the dough from the stand mixer. Shape it into a ball and place in a large bowl. Cover with a cloth and leave it to rise in the oven for 4 hours.

Divide the dough into 4 equal parts and shape 4 loaves. Place them on a floured cutting board and allow to rise for 30 minutes.

Spread each loaf using your hands, then use a rolling pin to flatten them into square pizzas, and trim them into 4 squares measuring 15 x 15 cm / 5.90 x 5.90 in each.

Roll the edges slightly and spread olive oil on the top. Preheat the oven to 200 °C / 392 °F and bake for 15 minutes.

Remove the pizzas from the oven, garnish them with sliced tomatoes and slices of bocconcini, drizzle with extra-virgin olive oil, add the shredded basil leaves and freshly crushed black peppercorns.

pomegranate and pistachio bulgur

4 servings
preparation: 15 min
cooking: 5 min
difficulty: easy

200 g / 7 oz bulgur
50 g / 1 ¾ oz raisins
1 ripe pomegranate
1 white onion
100 g / 3 ½ oz shelled, coarsely
chopped pistachios
100 g / 3 ½ oz feta cheese
walnut oil
olive oil
salt

Soak the raisins in lukewarm water for 30 minutes. Drain and set aside.

Clean the pomegranate and set the seeds aside in the refrigerator.

Heat 200 milliliters of water to a boil in a small saucepan. Remove from heat, add a little salt and add the bulgur.

Season with a tablespoon of walnut oil, cover and set aside for 15 minutes. Once the grains have absorbed the water and become compact, fluff them with a fork.

Dice the onion and cook it in a pan with a little olive oil until the onion starts to brown. Add the bulgur and stir, leaving it to sit for 5 minutes. Put 2/3 in one bowl and 1/3 in another.

In the bowl with 2/3 of the bulgur and onion, add the raisins and the pomegranate seeds. Add the pistachios and crumbled feta cheese to the bowl with 1/3 bulgur and onion.

Take 4 or 5 tablespoons of bulgur with raisins and arrange it on a dish. Flatten with a spatula and use a knife to shape it into a rectangle measuring 13 x 10 cm / 5.10 x 4 in. Take 2 tablespoons of bulgur with pistachios and arrange them along the short side of the first rectangle to make a rectangle measuring 13 x 4 cm / 5.10 x 1.60 in.

Prepare the other 3 portions the same way and serve.

tandoori chicken with basmati rice

6 servings
preparation: 30 min + resting time
cooking: 30 min
difficulty: challenging

tandoori chicken
400 g / 14 oz chicken breast
400 g / 14 oz natural yogurt
1 tsp chili pepper
1 tsp paprika
1 tsp nutmeg
1 tsp cumin powder
1 tsp coriander powder
½ tsp black peppercorns
½ tsp curcuma powder
red food coloring
2.5 cm / 1 in ginger
1 garlic clove
juice of 1 organic lemon
salt

papadams
150 g / 5 oz chickpea flour
1 tsp black sesame
½ tsp black peppercorns
½ tsp cayenne pepper
olive oil
salt

rice
200 g / 7 oz basmati rice
bunch of parsley

tandoori chicken
Grind the spices together with a mortar and pestle; add the food coloring, grated ginger and crushed clove of garlic. Pour the yogurt into a bowl, add spices and mix to obtain a homogeneous cream.

Cut the chicken into strips, sprinkle with lemon juice and submerge them in the yogurt cream. Add salt and allow to marinate in the refrigerator for 8 hours.

Line a baking sheet with baking paper. Drain the chicken of any excess yogurt sauce and set the marinade aside. Arrange the pieces on the baking sheet and bake in a preheated oven at 180 °C / 356 °F for 30 minutes. Baste the chicken frequently with the yogurt marinade throughout cooking.

papadams
Sift the flour, add the sesame, the black peppercorns and salt to taste. Stir and add enough water to make a soft, elastic dough. Knead the dough for 10 minutes, then divide it into 4 parts, flatten slightly and oil them on one side. Roll the dough and cut out 4 rectangles measuring 14 x 16 cm / 5.50 x 6.30 in. Dust slightly with cayenne pepper, place on a baking sheet lined with baking paper and cook for 30 minutes at 160 °C / 320 °F or until they are crisp.

rice
Put the rice in a strainer and rinse with cold water until the water runs clear. Strain, transfer to a bowl, cover with water and allow to rest for 30 minutes.

Transfer the rice in a pan with 500 ml / 16 fl oz of water. When the water boils, lower the heat and cook until the water is absorbed.

Place 4 strips of chicken on each papadam, arrange the rice, add a few leaves of chopped parsley and serve.

round meringue with wild strawberries

4 servings
preparation: 30 min
cooking: 3 h
difficulty: challenging

---

meringue
4 egg whites
100 g / 3 ½ oz granulated
sugar
100 g / 3 ½ oz confectioner's
sugar
1 tsp organic lemon juice
salt

topping
200 g / 7 oz wild strawberries
125 ml / 4 fl oz heavy cream

Place the egg whites in a deep bowl, add a pinch of salt and beat with an electric beater at medium speed. When they begin to form peaks, pour in the granulated sugar and lemon juice and continue to beat, increasing the speed, until the whites form stiff peaks.

Beating continuously, gradually add the sifted confectioner's sugar. When all the sugar has been incorporated and the mixture is stiff, smooth and shiny, the meringue is ready.

Line a pan with baking paper.

Fill a pastry bag set with a 2 cm / 0.80 in tip with the mixture and squeeze the meringue onto the baking paper using concentric movements to form a round base measuring 15 cm / 5.90 in in diameter. Using a star-shaped tip, make fifteen or so 1-cm / 0.40-in kisses.

Place the baking sheet in the oven at 90 °C / 194 °F and bake the meringues for 2 hours. Bake the base for an extra hour; the meringue should not cook, but rather dry out so it remains white. Set aside to cool.

Wash the wild strawberries and gently pat them dry with a paper towel. Whip the cream and put it in a pastry bag fitted with a 2 cm / 0.80 in star-shaped tip.

Distribute the cream on the base then arrange the strawberries on the upper semicircle and the meringue kisses on the lower semi-circle.

Delicious and **inviting**, magenta exerts a **youthful** and **sensual** force. **Provocative** and **passionate**, these red infused pinks set the table for **fun** and **festivities**.

magenta

tuna tartare and guacamole

4 servings
preparation: 50 min
no cooking
difficulty: medium

---

4 rectangular loaves of bread
corn chips

guacamole
2 avocados
1 spring onion
1 ripe tomato
juice of 1 organic lemon
Tabasco
salt

tuna tartare
400 g / 14 oz tuna fillet
1 organic blood orange
juice of 1 organic lemon
extra-virgin olive oil
dill, to taste
salt and pepper

guacamole
Eliminate the green parts of the spring onion and mince. Cut the tomato in half, remove seeds and cut into cubes.

Cut the avocados in half. Remove the pit and scrape the flesh out into a bowl with a spoon. Pour lemon juice over it and add a drop of Tabasco; then mash with a fork to create a creamy mixture.

Add the tomato and onion, stirring gently.

Cover the guacamole and leave in the refrigerator. Add salt to taste before serving.

tartare
Remove the orange zest, juice the orange and gradually whisk with the olive oil until emulsified.

Eliminate any dark flesh from the tuna, cut it into squares with a sharp knife. Put in a terrine and add the olive oil and lemon juice, then season with salt and pepper.

Spread one slice of bread with a layer of guacamole, then arrange the tartare on the upper part to create a rectangle, leaving a strip of guacamole on the lower part. Prepare 3 more pieces of bread the same way. Garnish with orange zest and dill, and serve with corn chips.

nigiri set

4 servings
preparation: 50 min
cooking: 40 min
difficulty: medium

200 g / 7 oz sushi rice
1 tsp kombu seaweed
30 ml / 1 fl oz rice vinegar
25 g / 1 oz sugar
10 g / ½ oz salt
sesame seeds

topping
fresh raw tuna
fresh raw salmon
red tobiko
orange tobiko
green tobiko
red lumpfish roe

fake nigiri
50 g / 1 ¾ oz tofu
nori seaweed

Rinse the rice under running water until it runs clear, removing excess starch.

Put the rice on a dishtowel and allow it to dry.

Pour the rice into a pan, cover it with water, add the seaweed and cook over medium heat for around 10 minutes, then lower the heat and continue to cook for 20 minutes. Turn off and set aside for 10 minutes.

Pour the rice vinegar into a small saucepan; add the sugar and salt, then heat to dissolve. Do not boil.

Remove the seaweed, pour the rice into a shallow casserole; add the sesame and the rice vinegar mixture and fluff the grains of rice. Cover with a cloth.

Cut the tuna and salmon into thin slices and then into squares measuring 3 x 3 cm / 1.20 x 1.20 in.

Wet your hands, take about 25 g / 1 oz of rice and mold it into rectangles measuring 4.5 x 3 cm / 1.80 x 1.20 in. Your rectangles should be 2.5 cm / 1 in thick.

Cut the tofu into 4 rectangles measuring 3 x 5 cm / 1.20 x 2 in, decorate them with a strip of nori seaweed.

Finish the nigiri sushi by arranging the squares of salmon and tuna, the different types of tobiko and the lumpfish eggs. Serve with the fake nigiri.

seared salmon with venere rice

4 servings
preparation: 20 min
cooking: 40 min
difficulty: easy

500 g / 1 lb salmon fillet
200 g / 7 oz Venere rice
whole pink peppercorns
extra-virgin olive oil
walnut oil
salt

Remove the skin from the salmon fillet and carefully check for any pin bones. Gently remove any that you find.

Heat a nonstick frying pan and quickly sear the salmon.

Cut the flesh into cubes with a sharp knife and drizzle a few drops of extra-virgin olive oil over it. Add some finely crushed pink peppercorns and salt to taste. Keep warm.

Boil the Venere rice in salted water, drain and season with walnut oil. Add salt if necessary.

Place about 2/3 tablespoons of rice on each dish. Using a knife, arrange it into 8 rectangles measuring 7 x 10 cm / 2.75 x 4 in each.

Using a lightly oiled square pastry cutter measuring 6 x 6 cm / 2.40 x 2.40 in, arrange the salmon on top of the rice, garnish with whole peppercorns and serve.

sea bream tartare with rose petals

4 servings
preparation: 30 min + resting time
no cooking
difficulty: medium

320 g / 11 ¼ oz sea bream fillet
½ shallot
2 green organic lemons
fleur de sel, to taste
pink peppercorns, to taste
80 g / 3 oz fromage blanc
20 g / ¾ oz horseradish cream
45 ml / 1 ½ fl oz extra-virgin
olive oil
20 rose petals
1 pomegranate

Place the sea bream fillets on a cutting board and, using a sharp knife, cut them into small cubes to make a tartare.

Cut the shallots into cubes and add to the tartare. Stir to combine gently, add the juice and grated zest of one lemon.

Drizzle with extra-virgin olive oil and dust with *fleur de sel* and crushed pink peppercorns.

Stir together gently, cover and refrigerate.

Put the *fromage blanc* in a bowl, add the juice and zest of the second lemon and whip with an electric beater. Add the horseradish cream, adjust the salt and work together to make a fluffy, foamy cream.

Clean the pomegranate and set the seeds aside in the refrigerator.

Wash the rose petals. Dry them, patting delicately with a paper towel, and cut into squares.

Put the cheese cream into a pastry bag and make a circle 6 cm / 2.40 in in diameter on a serving dish, then create a band measuring 2 x 4.5 cm / 0.80 x 1.80 in.

Take a little sea bream tartare at a time and arrange it around the cheese cream.

Once the 4 portions have been prepared, add the pomegranate seeds and the rose petals to the tartare and sprinkle with pink peppercorns.

Original recipe by Thierry Paludetto, Beefbar Monaco, Monte Carlo

cakesicles

6 servings
preparation: 40 min + resting time
cooking: 35 min
difficulty: medium

---

sponge cake
4 eggs
150 g / 5 oz granulated sugar
100 g / 3 ½ oz all-purpose flour
25 g / 1 oz potato starch
100 g / 3 ½ oz peach or apricot jam

decorations
300 g / 10 oz white chocolate
15 ml / ½ fl oz milk grated coconut
sugar stars, colored sugars, sugar strands, sugar pearl sprinkles…

To prepare the sponge cake, mix the eggs and the sugar together in a bowl. Whip the mixture with an electric beater at medium speed for 20 minutes to obtain a foamy, light-colored mixture.

Sift the flour with the starch, add them to the egg mixture delicately, using a whisk, raising the mixture up from the bottom, to avoid deflating the mixture.

Butter and flour a cake pan, pour the preparation into the pan, leveling the surface with a spatula and cook in an oven preheated to 170 °C / 338 °F for about 30 minutes, or until a toothpick poked into the center of the cake comes out dry and clean.

Turn off the oven and leave the sponge cake inside for 5 more minutes, then remove it and allow it to cool, crumble it into a bowl, add the jam and stir to create a compact consistency. Add more jam if necessary.

Using a 3 x 4 cm / 1.20 x 1.60 in pastry cutter, mold the mixture into rectangles at least 3 cm / 1.20 in high and insert the sticks at their base. Place the cake pops on a baking sheet, cover with plastic wrap and freeze for 30 minutes.

Melt the chocolate in a double boiler with a tablespoon of milk, quickly dip the cake pops in the chocolate, allow excess to drip off, lay them on a pastry cooling rack and place a 2 cm / 0.80 in square of baking paper on each. Dust the entire surface with grated coconut, remove the paper with tweezers and decorate with colored sugar, sprinkles or sugar stars in a rectangular shape.

Stick the cake pops into a polystyrene base or a piece of floral foam until the chocolate has hardened.

threesecake

4 servings
preparation: 45 min + resting time
no cooking
difficulty: challenging

crust

250 g / 8 oz graham cracker crumbs or similar biscuits
100 g / 3 ½ oz melted butter
40 g / 1 ¼ oz (1 ¼ oz Demerara sugar

cream

14 g / ½ oz sheets of gelatin
300 g / 10 oz fresh cream cheese
100 g / 3 ½ oz confectioner's sugar
30 ml / 1 fl oz drained sour cream
200 ml / 6 ¾ fl oz heavy cream
150 g / 5 oz strawberry fruit puree
150 g / 5 oz raspberry fruit puree
150 g / 5 oz blueberry fruit puree

sugar coated chocolate buttons

crust

Place the biscuits and sugar in a food processor and mix until completely crumbled; pour into a bowl, add the melted butter and stir to combine.

Line 3 square molds measuring 15 x 15 cm / 5.90 x 5.90 in with baking paper and divide the mixture evenly among them. Press with fingers to fill to a thickness of 1.5 cm / 0.60 in. Cover with plastic wrap and refrigerate for an hour.

cream

Filter the fruit purees with a strainer to remove seeds.

Mix the cheese, sour cream and confectioner's sugar with a whisk to create a creamy mixture.

Place the sheets of gelatin in cold water and soak for 10 minutes, then pat dry with a paper towel and allow them to dissolve in a bit of warm cream. Add this preparation to the cream, combine gently and carefully incorporate the whipped cream to produce a light, fluffy mixture.

Set half of the mixture aside, divide the other half into 3 bowls. Add the strawberry puree to the first, raspberry to the second and blueberry to the third.

Divide the 3 bases in 5 parts, cover each with the unflavored cream, level the surface with a spatula to produce a layer 0.50 cm / 0.20 in thick. Allow to set in the refrigerator for 30 minutes, then distribute a different fruit cream on each one. Put back in the refrigerator for another 30 minutes. Using a sharp knife, cut the last section of the fruit cream perpendicularly and delicately lift up, leaving the white section exposed. Add the sugar coated chocolate buttons.

Cover and allow to set in the refrigerator for 5 hours.

A hue that inspires awe with **mystery** and **intrigue**, purple is a distinctive shade range that demands **special attention**. The **uniqueness** inherent in this **extraordinary** color is highly preferred by those who are **artistic** and relish the idea of **not conforming**.

purple

cabbage with chickpeas dumplings

4 servings
preparation: 2 h and 30 min + resting time
cooking: 20 min
difficulty: easy

---

dumplings
300 g / 10 oz dried chickpeas
1 carrot
1 celery stalk
½ garlic clove
10 basil leaves
100 g / 3 ½ oz tofu
30 g / 1 oz kamut
breadcrumbs
grated zest of 1 organic lemon
extra-virgin olive oil
salt

salad
1 red cabbage
apple cider vinegar
raw unshelled pumpkin seeds,
to taste
raw unshelled sunflower
seeds, to taste
raisins, to taste
extra-virgin olive oil
salt

dumplings
Rinse the chickpeas under fresh water, and soak for 8 hours.

Put the soaked chickpeas in a pot with plenty of salted water, add the carrot and celery and simmer over low heat for 2 hours.

Drain and transfer to a blender with a little of the cooking water. Add the garlic, basil, cubes of tofu, 30 g / 1 oz of breadcrumbs and lemon zest. Season with a little extra-virgin olive oil and salt and mix to produce a creamy dense paste. If the paste is too dry, add a little of the cooking water; if it is too wet, add some breadcrumbs.

Shape the paste into nut-shaped balls and roll them in the breadcrumbs. Arrange them on a baking sheet lined with baking paper and cook for 20 minutes at 180 °C / 356 °F.

salad
Prepare the salad while the dumplings are cooking. Remove the outside leaves of the cabbage and the tough center core. Wash the leaves and pat them dry.

Slice the cabbage very thin, transfer it into a salad bowl and season with extra-virgin olive oil, apple cider vinegar, and salt. Cover and allow to rest in a cool place for 30 minutes.

Put 3–4 tablespoons of salad on a dish and, using a knife, arrange the salad into a rectangle measuring 12 x 8 cm / 4.70 x 3.15 in. Sprinkle with pumpkin and sunflower seeds, and a few raisins, creating a strip at the bottom with 10 dumplings.

beet and pumpkin ravioli

4 servings
preparation: 1 h + resting time
cooking: 25 min
difficulty: challenging

ravioli
500 g / 1 lb all-purpose flour
80 g / 3 oz durum wheat flour
2 eggs
2 tsp extra-virgin olive oil
(5 oz beets
200 g / 7 oz halved and
seeded pumpkin
salt

filling
250 g / 8 oz fresh cow ricotta
50 g / 1 ¾ oz grated
Parmigiano Reggiano
1 organic lemon
extra-virgin olive oil
salt and pepper

seasoning
butter
sage
black peppercorn

ravioli

Clean the beets and steam them, then peel and blend until they are a homogeneous puree.

Cook the pumpkin in the oven at 180 °C / 356 °F for 20 minutes, then cut into cubes and blend until it is a homogeneous puree.

Sift half of the flour into the bowl of a stand mixer. Mix with a dough hook and add a beaten egg, a pinch of salt, a teaspoonful of extra-virgin olive oil and the beet puree. Work for 15 minutes or until the dough is elastic and smooth and pulls away from the sides of the bowl. Once the dough is ready, gather it into a bowl, wrap in plastic wrap and set aside for 45 minutes.

Prepare the second ball of dough in the same way using the pumpkin puree.

filling

While the dough is resting, prepare the filling. Blend the grated Parmigiano Reggiano, the grated lemon zest, a stream of extra-virgin olive oil and season with salt and pepper.

Roll out each ball of dough into 2 thin sheets. Using a pastry bag, arrange nut-sized dollops of filling on the sheets, placing each dollop 4 cm / 1.60 in apart. Cover with the second sheet from the same ball of dough, press down the area surrounding the filling to remove air and push the 2 sheets together to seal them.

Cut the ravioli with the pastry wheel and place them on a floured board.

When all the ravioli are ready, boil them in a large pot of salted water and drain with a skimmer when they are *al dente*.

Drizzle the ravioli with melted butter and sage and dust with freshly crushed black peppercorns.

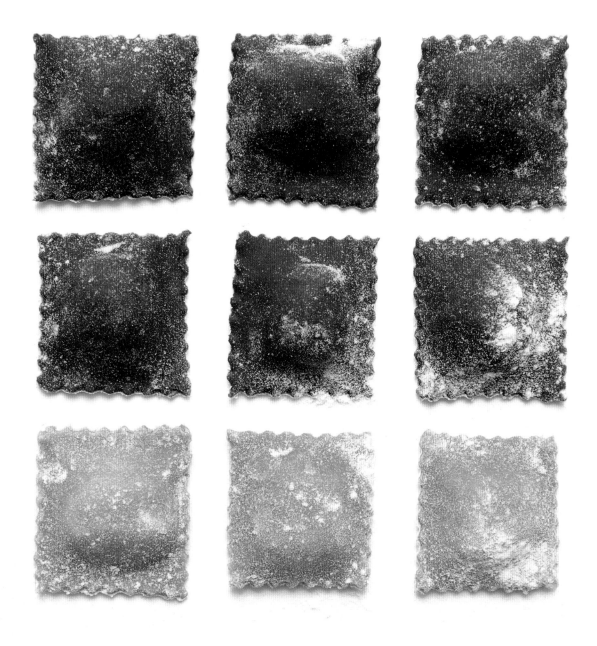

octopus salad with purple puree

4 servings
preparation: 30 min + resting time
cooking: 1 h
difficulty: medium

---

octopus salad
1 kg / 2 lb octopus
2 green celery stalks
extra-virgin olive oil, to taste
salt and pepper

puree
500 g / 1 lb purple potatoes
60 g / 2 oz butter
milk, to taste
salt

octopus
Wash the octopus, then plunge it into boiling water. Cover and cook at a simmer for at least 1 hour or until the flesh is tender. Drain and allow to cool.

Clean the celery and cut into rounds.

Drain the octopus and cut into small pieces. Transfer the octopus into a bowl, add the celery, drizzle with extra-virgin olive oil and add salt and pepper to taste.

puree
Boil the potatoes until tender. Drain. Peel and mash them into a saucepan with a potato ricer or masher.

Simmer over low heat to evaporate excess liquid while stirring. Add butter and enough milk to make a soft, smooth puree. Add salt to taste and allow to cool.

Place a round 14 cm / 5.50 in pastry cutter on a lightly oiled dinner plate. Arrange the octopus in the lower half, then place a piece of paper over the octopus in pastry cutter to avoid getting potatoes on the octopus while filling the form with potatoes.

Arrange the puree with a small-holed potato ricer, remove the paper and prepare the other 3 portions.

fox grape pudding

4 servings
preparation: 15 min + resting time
cooking: 25 min
difficulty: easy

___

pudding
800 g / 1 ¾ lb fox grapes (*Vitis labrusca*) or Concord grape
120 g / 4 oz Demerara sugar
40 g / 1 ¼ oz all-purpose flour
80 g / 3 oz potato starch

decoration
1 egg white granulated sugar
fox grapes (*Vitis labrusca*)
or Concord grape

Wash the grapes and put them in a pan. Add 300 milliliters of water and cook over low heat until it boils.

Continue to cook for 20 minutes, then put the grapes in a sieve and mash them to extract as much juice as possible.

Filter the juice, transfer it into a saucepan, add the sugar and the sifted flour and potato starch while stirring constantly. Slowly bring to a boil.

Continue to cook until the cream thickens and coats the spoon. If the pudding remains too liquid, add more potato starch.

Pour the pudding mixture into a mold to make a 3-cm / 1.20-in thick layer. Allow it to thicken for at least 6 hours.

Once the pudding has thickened, use a sharp knife to cut out 4 rectangles measuring 10 x 15 cm / 4 x 5.90 in each.

Dip the fox grapes in whipped egg white, then roll them in sugar and use them to decorate the pudding.

blueberry cheesecake

4 servings
preparation: 20 min + resting time
cooking: 30 min
difficulty: easy

---

crust
160 g / 5 ½ oz graham cracker
crumbs or similar biscuits
40 g / 1 ¼ oz Demerara sugar
80 g / 3 oz melted butter

filling
250 g / 8 oz fresh cream cheese
100 g / 3 ½ oz sugar
50 ml / 1 ¾ fl oz drained
sour cream
1 vanilla bean
salt

decoration
120 g / 4 oz blueberries

crust
Place the biscuits and sugar in a food processor and mix until completely crumbled; pour into a bowl, add the melted butter and stir to combine.

Line a baking sheet with baking paper then, using an expandable cake frame, create a 16 cm x 16 cm / 6.30 x 6.30 in frame. Pour in the biscuit mixture, spread evenly, press firmly onto the bottom and up the sides of the pan to form an approximately 2-cm / 0.80-in-high rim. Cover with plastic wrap and refrigerate for an hour.

filling
Cream the cheese with a whisk or electric beater on low speed for 10 minutes, add a pinch of salt, sugar and continue to whip the cream for 10 minutes.

Add the drained sour cream, the vanilla bean seeds and blend to create a fluffy and homogeneous cream.

Pour the cream over the base and smooth the surface with a spatula. Cover and refrigerate for 3 hours.

Before serving, remove the cheesecake from its frame and decorate 2/3 of the top with blueberries.

The color of the **sky** and the **sea**, blue is the most dominant color of our **natural habitat** and is a **universal favorite**. **Dependable**, **consoling** and **constant**, we crave the **quiet calm** and **peace** blue provides.

blue

salad with borage flowers

4 servings
preparation: 10 min
cooking: 10 min
difficulty: easy

---

frittata
2 eggs
25 g / 1 oz grated Parmigiano
Reggiano cheese
2 sprigs of mint leaves
butter
salt

salad
mesclun salad
mâche salad
potentilla flowers
mint leaves
dill
sliced almonds
borage flowers

citronette
100 ml / 3 ½ fl oz extra-virgin
olive oil
1 organic lemon
chives, to taste
black peppercorns

frittata
To prepare the frittata, break the eggs into a large bowl, add the Parmigiano Reggiano, salt to taste, add the chopped mint, and beat with a fork or whisk.

Heat a nonstick pan, melt the butter and pour in the eggs. Cook the frittata covered over low heat for 5 minutes, slipping a spatula under the edge to free the frittata from the pan.

Turn the frittata and slide it back into the pan.

Continue cooking for 5 minutes, transfer to a cutting board and cut into mini frittatas using a round pastry cutter measuring 4 cm / 1.60 in in diameter.

salad
Carefully wash the salad, arrange it on the dishes, creating a circle measuring 12 cm / 4.70 in in diameter. Garnish with the almonds and borage flowers and set aside.

citronette
Pour the extra-virgin olive oil into a jar with a cover, add the grated lemon zest, chopped chives and freshly crushed black peppercorns. Close the cover and shake to emulsify the ingredients.

Dress salad with the citronette and serve with the frittata.

blue cabbage risotto and green apple

4 servings
preparation: 15 min
cooking: 30 min
difficulty: easy

240 g / 8 ¼ oz superfino rice
(Arborio)
400 g / 14 oz red cabbage
1 shallot
1 l vegetable broth
blue natural food coloring
30 g / 1 oz butter grated
Parmigiano Reggiano cheese
1 granny smith apple
juice of 1 organic lemon
rosemary
60 ml / 2 fl oz extra-virgin olive
oil
salt

Clean the cabbage, cut into strips and sweat off in a pan with a tablespoon of extra-virgin olive oil for 10 minutes or until the cabbage is wilted. Transfer the cabbage to the bowl of a food processor, add a little olive oil and water and blend to produce a smooth, homogeneous cream.

Slice the shallots thin. Heat 2 tablespoons of extra-virgin olive oil in a pan, add the sliced shallots and cook until they are translucent.

Add the rice, stir and cook until the grains of rice are shiny and translucent, then add 2 ladlefuls of boiling broth and continue to add more as it evaporates. About halfway through cooking add the cabbage cream, a few drops of food coloring and salt to taste.

Cook the risotto *al dente*, remove from heat and stir in the butter and some Parmigiano Reggiano. Allow the risotto to amalgamate for 5 minutes.

Cut the apple into small cubes, sprinkle with lemon juice and set aside.

Place a 5 x 7 cm / 2 x 2.75 in pastry cutter on a serving dish, fill it with risotto until it is 2 cm / 0.80 in thick. Prepare 8 portions in the same manner.

Arrange the apple cubes on the rice, sprinkle with finely cut rosemary and serve.

sablé tart with anchovies

4 servings
preparation: 45 min + resting time
cooking: 20 min
difficulty: medium

sablé tart
200 g / 7 oz salted whole grain crackers
80 g / 3 oz butter

marinated anchovies
500 g / 1 lb small anchovy fillets
strained juice of 6 large organic lemons
salt and pepper

topping
sun-dried tomatoes in olive oil, to taste
thyme, to taste
pine nuts, to taste
wild fennel leaves, to taste

Cook the pine nuts in a nonstick pan until they are lightly toasted. Remove any that have become too dark. Allow them to cool and set aside.

sablé tart
Put the crackers in a food processor and blend until they are finely crumbled, then pour into a bowl, add melted butter and stir.

Transfer the mixture into a rectangular pan lined with baking paper and press well to level the surface. Cover and refrigerate for 3 hours.

marinated anchovies
Clean the anchovies by removing the heads and innards. Open the fillets down the spine and remove the bones, then wash thoroughly under running water and pat dry with a paper towel.

Place the anchovy fillets in a single layer in a dish, skin side down. Add salt, pepper and marinate, completely covering with strained lemon juice. Cover and refrigerate for 2 hours.

Delicately cut the base into 4 rectangles measuring 13 x 17 cm / 5.10 x 6.70 in each, arrange the anchovy fillets, chopped sun-dried tomatoes and thyme leaves on a square measuring 10 x 10 cm / 4 x 4 in. At the bottom, arrange a row of toasted pine nuts, dust with chopped wild fennel leaves and serve.

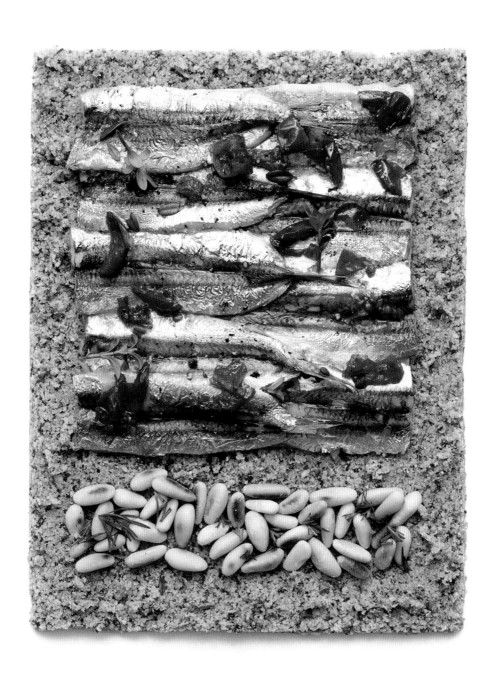

bluebird and robin biscuits

4 servings
preparation: 20 min + resting time
cooking: 15 min
difficulty: easy

200 g / 7 oz all-purpose flour
100 g / 3 ½ oz butter
100 g / 3 ½ oz confectioner's
sugar
2 egg yolks
grated zest of 1 small organic
lemon
1 pinch of salt
honey

decoration
nonpareils
colored sugar crystals

To prepare the shortbread dough, wash the lemon and grate the zest into a bowl.

Sift the flour into a mound with a well in the center, put the softened butter in the middle with a pinch of salt. Combine the ingredients using fingertips to create large crumbs.

Form a new well and put the yolks in the center with the sugar and lemon zest.

Work the ingredients into the dough using fingertips to create a smooth dough. Collect it into a ball, wrap with plastic wrap and refrigerate for at least an hour.

Roll out the dough to 0.50 cm / 0.20 in thick. Using 2 rectangular pastry cutters, cut out the biscuits in 2 different sizes measuring 3 x 5 cm / 1.20 x 2 in and 4 x 5 cm / 1.60 x 2 in each.

Place the biscuits on a baking sheet lined with baking paper and bake at 180 °C / 356 °F for 15 minutes or until the biscuits are light gold.

Remove from the oven and allow to cool on a cooling rack.

Once the biscuits have cooled, take one at a time and place a strip of paper 1 cm / 0.40 in wide on the lower part. Brush each biscuit with a thin layer of honey and decorate with nonpareils and colored sugar crystals.

donuts

4 servings
preparation: 30 min + resting time
cooking: 20 min
difficulty: challenging

---

donuts
7 g / ¼ oz dry yeast
500 g / 1 lb flour 0
240 ml / 8 fl oz milk
60 g / 2 oz butter
3 egg yolks
25 g / 1 oz sugar
½ tsp cinnamon powder
sunflower oil
salt

glaze
200 g / 7 oz confectioner's
sugar
50 ml / 1 ¾ fl oz milk
light blue and blue natural
food coloring

decoration
sugar stars
sugar strands
sugar pearls
sprinkles

donuts
Dissolve the yeast in lukewarm water and allow it to rest for 5 minutes.

Put the flour, milk, softened butter, egg yolks, sugar, yeast, cinnamon and a pinch of salt in the bowl of a stand mixer. Mix with the dough hook and knead for 10 minutes, then transfer into a lightly greased bowl, cover with a cloth and set in a warm place to rise for 2 hours or until it doubles in volume.

Put the dough on a lightly-floured board and flatten it with your hands to about 1.5 cm / 0.60 in.

Cut 8 donuts using a cookie cutter measuring 7 cm / 6.70 in in diameter, then use a smaller one to cut out the hole. Transfer them onto a cutting board and set to rise for 45 minutes or until they have doubled in volume.

Heat a deep fryer, or a large saucepan, filled with sunflower oil to 175–180 °C / 347–356 °F and fry the donuts in small batches (max 2 at a time) turning over frequently with a spider strainer. When ready, transfer the fried donuts to a cooling rack and allow to cool slightly.

glaze
Prepare the glaze while the donuts are cooling. Dissolve the confectioner's sugar in milk, set aside 3 spoonfuls of white glaze; divide the rest into 2 bowls and mix in the food coloring.

Dip one side of the donuts into the colored glaze and set to dry on the cooling rack. Dip the tip of a brush in the white glaze and move it to create a 2-cm / 0.80-in-wide zigzag strip. Sprinkle with your choice of decorations and serve when the glaze is set.

PANTONE
UNIVERSE
2728

Symbolic of **good health**, greens are associated with **growth**, **fertility** and the **environment**. greens can quickly bring about a sense of **balance** and **harmony**, causing us to **breathe slowly** and **deeply**, helping the heart **relax**.

green

PANTONE
UNIVERSE™
376 C

PANTONE
UNIVERSE™
585 C

pureed spinach + creamed peas

4 servings
preparation: 10 min
cooking: 20 min (pureed spinach), 30 min (creamed peas)
difficulty: easy

pureed spinach
1.5 kg / 3 lb fresh spinach
75 g / 3 oz butter
½ white onion
1 garlic clove
250 ml / 8 fl oz vegetable broth
200 ml / 6 ¾ fl oz heavy cream
nutmeg
extra-virgin olive oil
salt

creamed peas
500 g / 1 lb peas
1 shallot
2 lettuce leaves
1 leek
1 potato
250 ml / 8 fl oz vegetable broth
extra-virgin olive oil

pureed spinach

Clean and wash spinach. Put it in a saucepan, add a glass of water and boil for 10 minutes. Once cooked, drain spinach and squeeze out excess water, then transfer to processor and blend until smooth. Add salt if necessary.

Melt butter in heavy-bottomed medium saucepan over medium heat, add the chopped onion and garlic and sauté until browned. Add the spinach puree, pour in the hot broth and bring to a boil.

Add the cream and a dusting of nutmeg, continue cooking over low heat for 10 minutes.

Transfer the cream into dishes. Drizzle with extra-virgin olive oil and serve with salted biscuits (see recipe on opposite page).

creamed peas

Heat 2 tablespoons of extra-virgin olive oil in a saucepan, add shallot sliced into thin rings and sauté. Add the peas and lettuce, then add the leeks sliced into circles and the potato cut into cubes.

Cover with hot vegetable broth and cook for 30 minutes, mix with an immersion blender to obtain a smooth homogeneous cream. If the cream is too thick, add more broth to have the desired consistency.

Transfer the puree into dishes. Drizzle with extra-virgin olive oil and serve with salted biscuits (see recipe on opposite page).

cream of asparagus + salted biscuits

4 servings
preparation: 10 min + resting time
cooking: 40 min
difficulty: easy

---

cream of asparagus
1 kg / 2 lb asparagus
2 potatoes
1 leek
50 ml / 1 ¾ fl oz heavy cream
extra-virgin olive oil
salt and pepper

pâte brisée
150 g / 5 oz all-purpose flour
75 g / 2 ½ oz salted butter
15 ml / ½ fl oz oregano

cheese cream
50 g / 1 ¾ oz cream cheese
25 g / 1 oz Greek yogurt
1 bunch chives

anchovy fillets in olive oil
15 ml / ½ fl oz lemon zest
semi-cured goat cheese
chopped walnuts
black peppercorns

Prepare the *pâte brisée* for the salted biscuits and the cheese cream following the recipe on page 80.

Clean the asparagus, discard their fibrous ends, then rinse them under water to eliminate any remaining dirt.

Cut the asparagus into pieces and put in a pot. Add the sliced leek and cubed potatoes. Add 600 milliliters of water, salt to taste and slowly bring to a boil. Cover and lower the heat and allow to simmer for 30 minutes.

While waiting for the cream of asparagus to cook, take at least 12 biscuits. Using square pastry cutter measuring 3 x 3 cm / 1.20 x 1.20 in, garnish 4 with the cheese cream spread, 4 with the anchovy fillets and lemon zest, and the remaining 4 with goat cheese squares, chopped walnuts and crushed black peppercorns. Set aside.

Use an immersion blender to puree the asparagus and mix with the cooking liquid to produce a smooth, homogeneous cream. Return to the cook top and add the cream, then continue to cook for 10 minutes over low heat.

Divide the cream of asparagus among 4 bowls, drizzle with olive oil and crushed pepper and serve with the salted biscuits.

mezzemaniche with broccoli and ricotta

4 servings
preparation: 30 min
cooking: 20 min
difficulty: challenging

---

200 g / 7 oz mezzemaniche
1 purple cauliflower
400 g / 14 oz broccoli florets
30 g / 1 oz grated Parmigiano
Reggiano cheese
60 ml / 2 fl oz extra-virgin olive
oil
salt

filling
40 g / 1 ¼ oz cow ricotta
40 g / 1 ¼ oz sheep ricotta
light olive oil

Clean the purple cauliflower and break down into florets. Wash them under running water and blanch for 5 minutes. Drain and transfer immediately into a bowl of ice water. After 2 minutes, drain and set florets aside in a bowl.

Rinse the broccoli florets, blanch for 5 minutes and place in ice water. After 2 minutes, drain and set aside in a bowl.

Set aside 10 broccoli florets and put the remaining broccoli in a food processor. Add the Parmigiano Reggiano, extra-virgin olive oil and mix to produce a smooth cream. Add salt to taste and set aside.

To prepare the filling, mix the ricotta with 2 or 3 tablespoons of light olive oil.

Crumble the cauliflower and broccoli florets you set aside earlier and prepare 2 bases side by side one measuring 14 x 10 cm / 5.50 x 4 in, the other 14 x 4 cm / 5.50 x 1.60 in.

Fill one pastry bag with the creamed broccoli and another with the ricotta cream.

Cook the pasta *al dente*, and fill them with the 2 creams, standing the pipes on end. Serve immediately.

pork loin with sesame seeds

4 servings
preparation: 15 min
cooking: 40 min
difficulty: easy

---

12 boneless pork loin chops
30 ml / 1 fl oz maple syrup
white sesame seeds
wasabi sesame seeds
black sesame seeds
extra-virgin olive oil
salt

quince jam
500 g / 1 lb quinces
300 g / 10 oz Demerara sugar
juice of 1 organic lemon
white sesame seeds, to taste

Roughly cut up the quinces without peeling, place them in a heavy-bottomed saucepan, add a glass of cold water and cook for 30 minutes or until they come apart.

Run the quinces through a ricer or food mill into a saucepan. Add sugar and lemon juice, and cook, stirring occasionally for about 40 minutes.

Put the quince jam in a jar, add the sesame seeds, stir and allow to cool.

Trim the loin chops with a sharp knife to remove any fat and pound slightly until the meat is 0.50 cm / 0.20 in thick.

Heat a tablespoon of extra-virgin olive oil in a nonstick pan and cook the slices for 10 minutes. Add the maple syrup, turn the meat over and cook for another 5 minutes.

On a cutting board, slice the meat into a dozen 6 x 7 cm / 2.40 x 2.75 in rectangles.

Transfer the meat onto a cutting board, salt to taste, sprinkle with sesame seeds, arrange on plates with the quince jam and serve.

savory asparagus tarts

4 servings
preparation: 40 min + resting time
cooking: 40 min
difficulty: medium

---

2 bunches asparagus
2 puff pastry sheets
Edam cheese, to taste
salt and pepper

cheese béchamel
25 g / 1 oz butter
25 g / 1 oz all-purpose flour
250 ml / 8 fl oz milk
25 g / 1 oz Emmental cheese
nutmeg

Clean the asparagus, discard their fibrous ends. Rinse them under water to eliminate any remaining dirt, parboil in boiling salted water for 2 minutes and set aside.

To prepare the béchamel, melt the butter in a heavy-bottomed saucepan and add the sifted flour, stirring constantly, until the mixture begins to foam.

Remove from heat and, stirring constantly, add hot milk, salt to taste and add thinly sliced Emmental cheese. Return to heat and cook for about 10 minutes. Once ready, flavor with nutmeg to taste and keep warm.

Roll out the puff pastry and cut 4 rectangles measuring 12 x 17 cm / 4.70 x 6.70 in each. Pour the cheese béchamel on top of them, leaving an edge.

Arrange the asparagus on each tart and bake in the oven at 180 °C / 356 °F for 30 minutes.

Once cooked, allow the savory tarts to cool slightly, garnish with a thin strip of Edam cheese, sprinkle with pepper and serve.

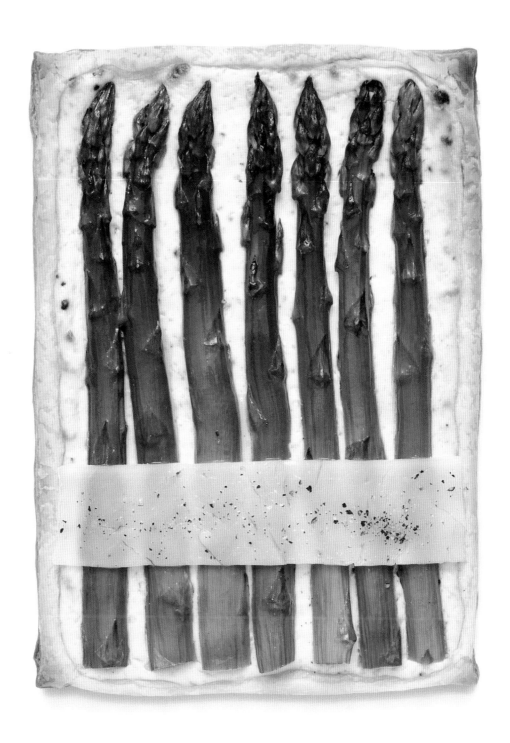

spinach and pine nut long cake

4 servings
preparation: 1 h
cooking: 1 h
difficulty: medium

---

cake
500 g / 1 lb fresh spinach
3 eggs
30 g / 1 oz grated Parmigiano
Reggiano cheese
100 g / 3 ½ oz pine nuts
nutmeg
Parmigiano Reggiano flakes,
to taste

béchamel
25 g / 1 oz butter
25 g / 1 oz all-purpose flour
250 ml / 8 fl oz milk
nutmeg
salt and pepper

béchamel
Melt the butter in a heavy-bottomed saucepan and add the sifted flour, stirring constantly, until the mixture begins to foam.

Remove from heat and, stirring constantly, add hot milk, salt to taste. Return to heat and cook for about 10 minutes. Once ready, add nutmeg to taste.

cake
Clean the spinach and put it in a saucepan without draining. Cook for 10 minutes, then drain and allow to cool.

Squeeze excess water from the spinach and chop into large pieces, then add them to the béchamel.

Stir, add the eggs, grated Parmigiano Reggiano, 25 g / 1 oz of pine nuts and flavor with nutmeg to taste.

Butter a mold and pour the spinach mixture in. Level off the surface, place some whole pine nuts on top and cook over water in the oven at 180 °C / 356 °F for 45 minutes.

Once the cake has cooled, remove from mold and cut 4 rectangular cakes measuring 20 x 4 cm / 7.9 x 1.60 in each. Garnish the lower part with the remaining pine nuts and Parmigiano Reggiano flakes.

pistachio green cakes

4 servings
preparation: 45 min
cooking: 30 min
difficulty: medium

---

sponge cake
4 eggs
150 g / 5 oz granulated sugar
100 g / 3 ½ oz flour
25 g / 1 oz potato starch
25 g / 1 oz chopped pistachios

cream
250 g / 8 oz creamy robiola
cheese
150 g / 5 oz mascarpone
cheese
100 g / 3 ½ oz confectioner's
sugar
30 g / 1 oz pistachio powder
100 g / 3 ½ oz pistachio
crumbs

sponge cake
Put eggs and sugar in a bowl and whip with an electric beater at medium speed for 20 minutes or until the mixture has lightened and is thick and foamy.

Sift the flour and potato starch together and gently fold the flour into the egg mixture using a whisk to stir from the bottom up. Gently fold the chopped pistachios into the batter.

Butter and flour a jelly roll pan, pour in the batter, level the surface with a spatula and cook in a preheated oven at 170 °C / 338 °F for about 30 minutes, or until a toothpick inserted in the center comes out clean.

Turn off the oven and allow the sponge cake to rest for 5 minutes. Remove from oven and allow to cool completely.

cream
Put the robiola and the mascarpone cheese in a bowl and add the confectioner's sugar, the pistachio powder and mix with an electric beater until the mixture is light and creamy.

Using a pastry cutter, cut the cake into 16 squares measuring 5 x 5 cm / 2 x 2 in each.

Distribute the cream on the sponge cakes, sculpting it with a knife. Garnish the upper section of the cakes with the pistachio crumbs and refrigerate until serving time.

guidelines

When it comes to creativity, it often seems difficult to follow strict guidelines. But even the most enjoyable games have rules. Those we applied while designing our recipes were born of the proportions of the Pantone Chip, a relationship of percentages and standard distances that must be followed in order to achieve the final effect. The ingredients and their quantities were added a little in abundance, in order to allow our readers to make mistakes or interpret the Pantone "canon" according to their own desires.

For rectangular and/or square Chips, we adhered to a 3:4 proportion. For rounded Chips, 2:3. When a color fills a space, it is centered and set apart by the same distances on at least 3 sides. Where to put an "ingredient-color," where not to put one, which texture to use in laying them out… All this you can decide on your own. You don't have to be an architect: all measurements and tools can be adapted, reviewed, reconsidered according to your own personal vision.

These recipes may inspire many others, all bound by the same simple formula: "the right taste in the right shape and the right color."

SKETCHES

RYE BREAD APPETIZERS

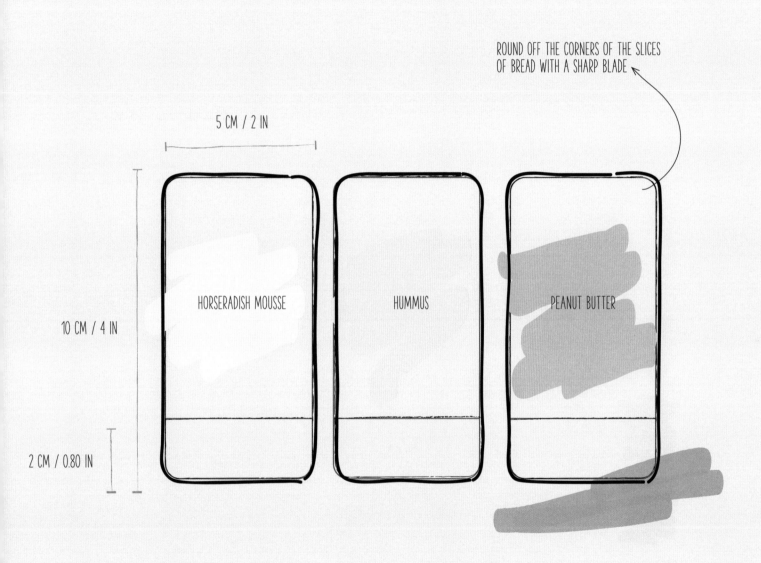

ROUND OFF THE CORNERS OF THE SLICES OF BREAD WITH A SHARP BLADE

5 CM / 2 IN

10 CM / 4 IN

2 CM / 0.80 IN

HORSERADISH MOUSSE

HUMMUS

PEANUT BUTTER

COARSE YELLOW
CORNMEAL

 SQUID INK

 GREEN PEPPER

 RED PEPPER

BUMBLEBEE POLENTA

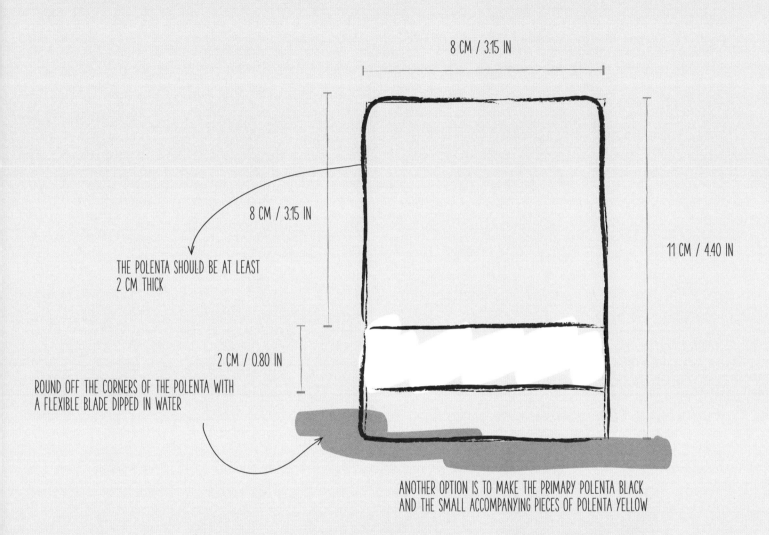

8 CM / 3.15 IN

8 CM / 3.15 IN

THE POLENTA SHOULD BE AT LEAST
2 CM THICK

11 CM / 4.40 IN

2 CM / 0.80 IN

ROUND OFF THE CORNERS OF THE POLENTA WITH
A FLEXIBLE BLADE DIPPED IN WATER

ANOTHER OPTION IS TO MAKE THE PRIMARY POLENTA BLACK
AND THE SMALL ACCOMPANYING PIECES OF POLENTA YELLOW

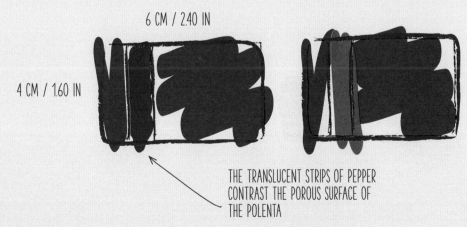

6 CM / 2.40 IN

4 CM / 1.60 IN

THE TRANSLUCENT STRIPS OF PEPPER
CONTRAST THE POROUS SURFACE OF
THE POLENTA

ONION

SAFFRON PISTILS

FOR A STYLIZED EFFECT, ARRANGE THE DISH WITH A
MINIMALIST DECORATION CREATED WITH A SQUARE
OF ONION AND A SAFFRON PISTIL

RISOTTO WITH PARMIGIANO TUILES

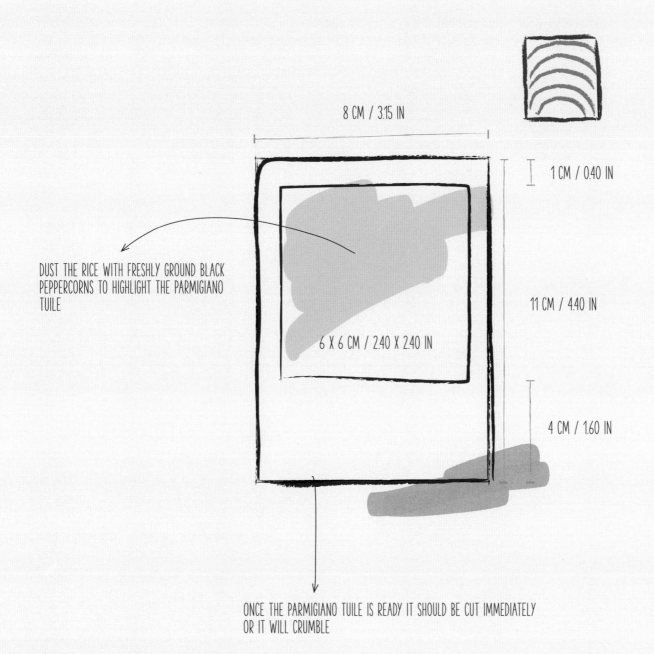

8 CM / 3.15 IN

1 CM / 0.40 IN

11 CM / 4.40 IN

4 CM / 1.60 IN

6 X 6 CM / 2.40 X 2.40 IN

DUST THE RICE WITH FRESHLY GROUND BLACK PEPPERCORNS TO HIGHLIGHT THE PARMIGIANO TUILE

ONCE THE PARMIGIANO TUILE IS READY IT SHOULD BE CUT IMMEDIATELY OR IT WILL CRUMBLE

TRUFFLED QUAIL EGGS

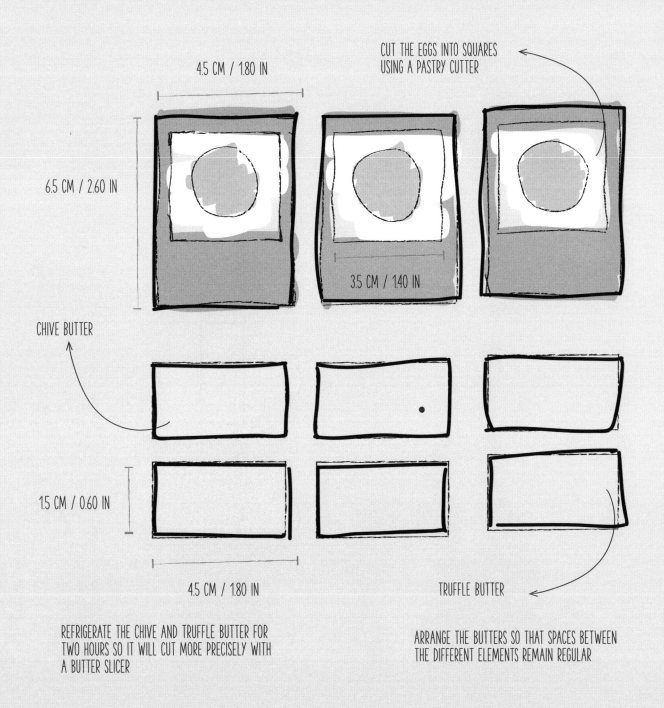

4.5 CM / 1.80 IN

CUT THE EGGS INTO SQUARES
USING A PASTRY CUTTER

6.5 CM / 2.60 IN

3.5 CM / 1.40 IN

CHIVE BUTTER

1.5 CM / 0.60 IN

4.5 CM / 1.80 IN

TRUFFLE BUTTER

REFRIGERATE THE CHIVE AND TRUFFLE BUTTER FOR
TWO HOURS SO IT WILL CUT MORE PRECISELY WITH
A BUTTER SLICER

ARRANGE THE BUTTERS SO THAT SPACES BETWEEN
THE DIFFERENT ELEMENTS REMAIN REGULAR

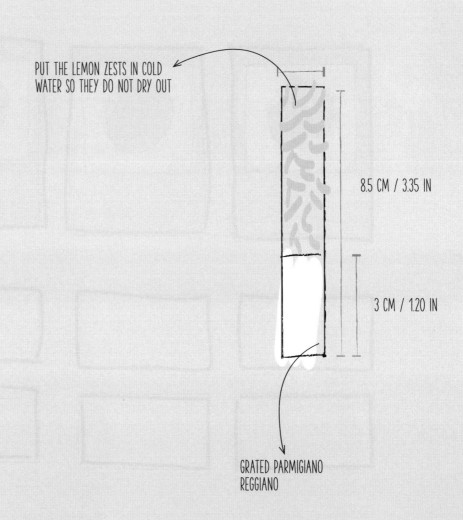

PUT THE LEMON ZESTS IN COLD
WATER SO THEY DO NOT DRY OUT

8.5 CM / 3.35 IN

3 CM / 1.20 IN

GRATED PARMIGIANO
REGGIANO

LEMON LINGUINE

FOR AN ORIGINAL TOUCH, DECORATE THE TABLE WITH A STRIP OF LEMON ZEST AND GRATED PARMESAN

PEAS   +   CORN KERNELS   +   CARROTS

ALTERNATIVES

BLACK OLIVES   +   BEETS   +   TOMATO

DECONSTRUCTED RUSSIAN SALAD

CUT THE EGGS AT THE BASE SO THEY STAND UP

TO CUT THE EGGS PRECISELY
IN HALF USE A COTTON THREAD
AND TIGHTEN IT FIRMLY AROUND
THE EGG LIKE A BELT

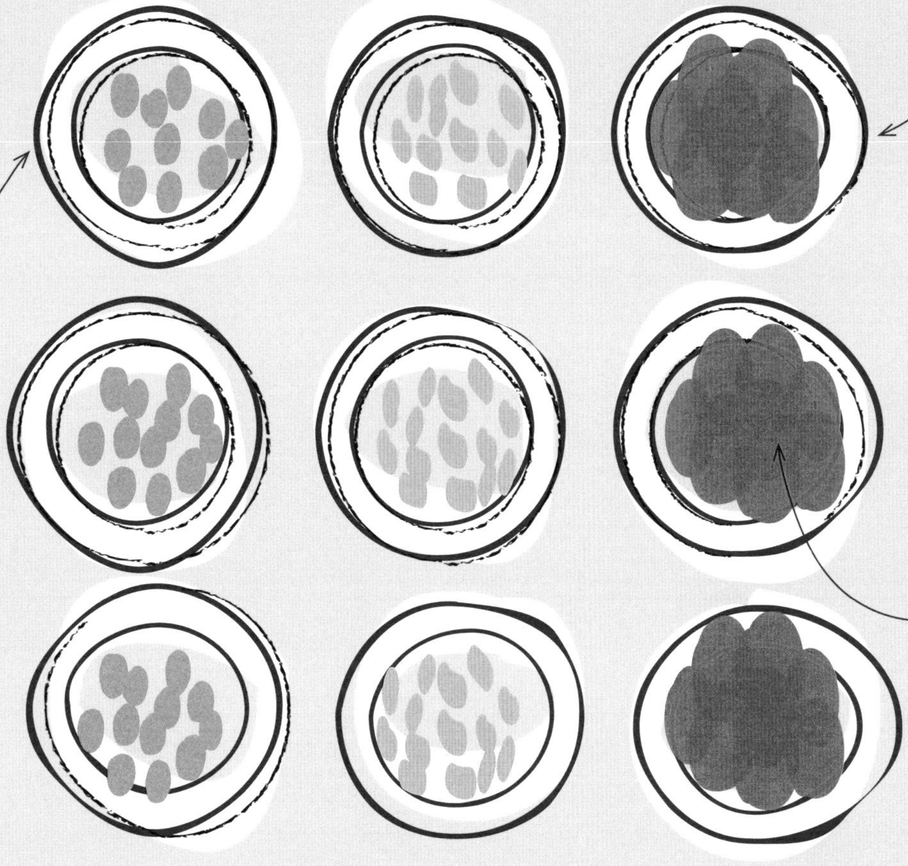

DECORATE WITH PEAS, CORN
KERNELS, CARROT CIRCLES OR
SLICED BLACK OLIVES, DICED BEETS,
DICED TOMATOES

SERVE THE SALAD ON A SQUARE, COLORED SURFACE (SUCH AS A PAPER NAPKIN)
FRAMING THE COMPOSITION OF ROUND ELEMENTS: EGGS, PEAS, CORN KERNELS,
CARROT CIRCLES

26

MANGO PUDDING WITH PANNA COTTA

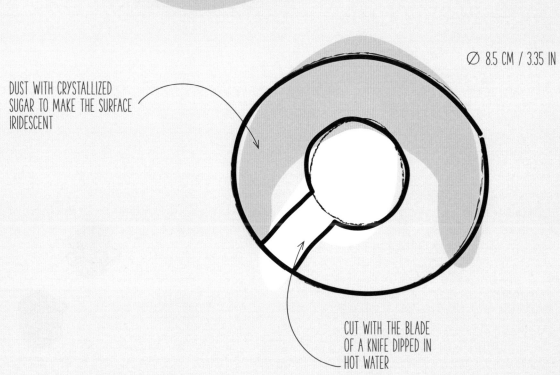

1.5 CM / 0.60 IN

2.5 CM / 1 IN

ARRANGE THE PUDDINGS ON A SERVING DISH IN DIFFERENT POSITIONS WITH RESPECT TO ONE ANOTHER

TO CUT THE MANGO PUDDING USE A PASTRY CUTTER AND KNIFE DIPPED IN HOT WATER

⌀ 3.5 CM / 1.40 IN

DUST WITH CRYSTALLIZED SUGAR TO MAKE THE SURFACE IRIDESCENT

⌀ 8.5 CM / 3.35 IN

CUT WITH THE BLADE OF A KNIFE DIPPED IN HOT WATER

DECORATE THE SERVING DISH
WITH A FEW RASPBERRIES

TARTE CITRON

15 CM / 5.90 IN

10 CM / 4 IN

5 CM / 2 IN

IN ORDER TO GET A PERFECT CRUST,
BLIND BAKE THE PIE USING DRIED
LEGUMES OR CERAMIC PIE WEIGHTS.
THIS PREVENTS THE DOUGH FROM RISING
WHILE BAKING

ARRANGE THE MERINGUES USING
TONGS

ONION   CUCUMBER   YELLOW PEPPER   RED PEPPER

GAZPACHO

ACCOMPANY THE DISH WITH DICED RAW
INGREDIENTS ARRANGED IN A RECTANGLE

SOAK THE DICED ONION IN WATER
TO SWEETEN IT

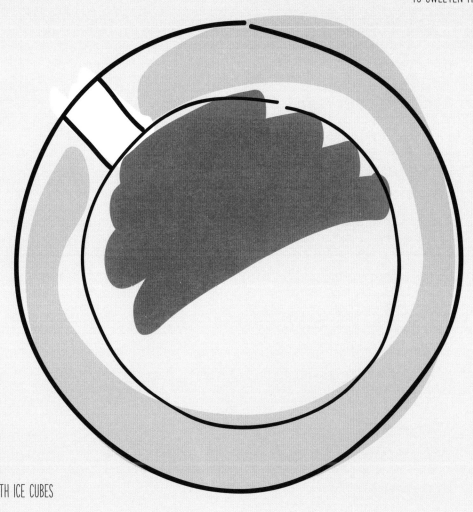

THE GAZPACHO MAY BE GARNISHED WITH ICE CUBES
ADDED JUST BEFORE SERVING

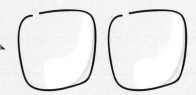

CHEDDAR WITH AROMATIC JAMS

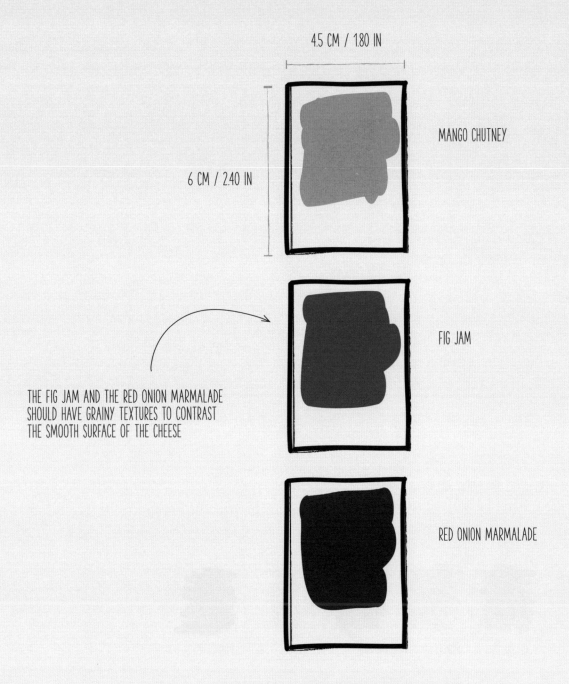

4.5 CM / 1.80 IN

6 CM / 2.40 IN

MANGO CHUTNEY

FIG JAM

THE FIG JAM AND THE RED ONION MARMALADE
SHOULD HAVE GRAINY TEXTURES TO CONTRAST
THE SMOOTH SURFACE OF THE CHEESE

RED ONION MARMALADE

ARRANGE THE CHEDDAR RECTANGLES PRECISELY IN A GRID

TO VARY THE TEXTURE OF THE SALAD, INCLUDE RADICCHIO,
AND DRIED AND FRESH FRUIT CUT INTO EQUAL PIECES

PARMIGIANO   WALNUTS   FRITTATA   ORANGE   PINK GRAPEFRUIT   RADICCHIO
REGGIANO
SHAVINGS

FRITTATA WITH RADICCHIO & WALNUT SALAD

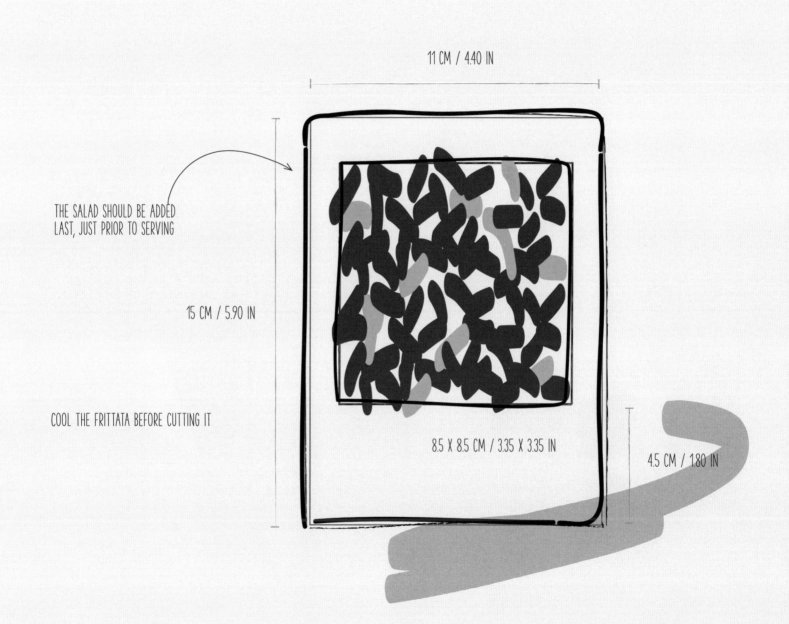

11 CM / 4.40 IN

THE SALAD SHOULD BE ADDED
LAST, JUST PRIOR TO SERVING

15 CM / 5.90 IN

COOL THE FRITTATA BEFORE CUTTING IT

8.5 X 8.5 CM / 3.35 X 3.35 IN

4.5 CM / 1.80 IN

RED MULLET FILLETS

SWEET POTATOES

RED MULLET FLESH

RED MULLET ON SWEET POTATO

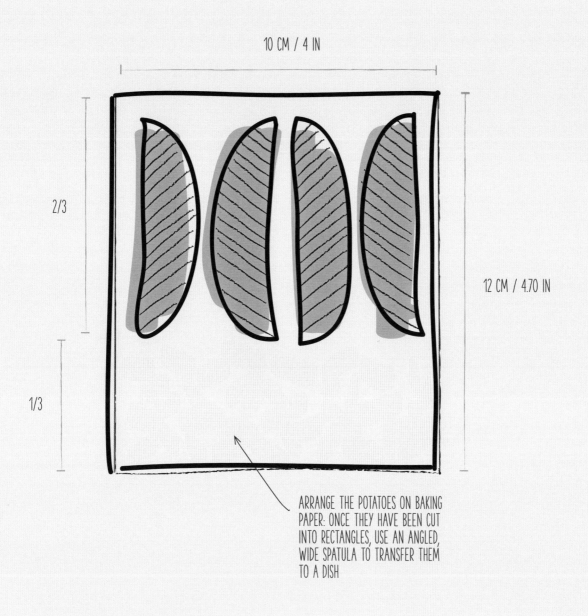

10 CM / 4 IN

12 CM / 4.70 IN

2/3

1/3

ARRANGE THE POTATOES ON BAKING
PAPER: ONCE THEY HAVE BEEN CUT
INTO RECTANGLES, USE AN ANGLED,
WIDE SPATULA TO TRANSFER THEM
TO A DISH

USE A WELL-SHARPENED, LONG, STRAIGHT
KNIFE TO TRIM THE BED OF POTATOES

CARROT SALAD WITH KEFTA

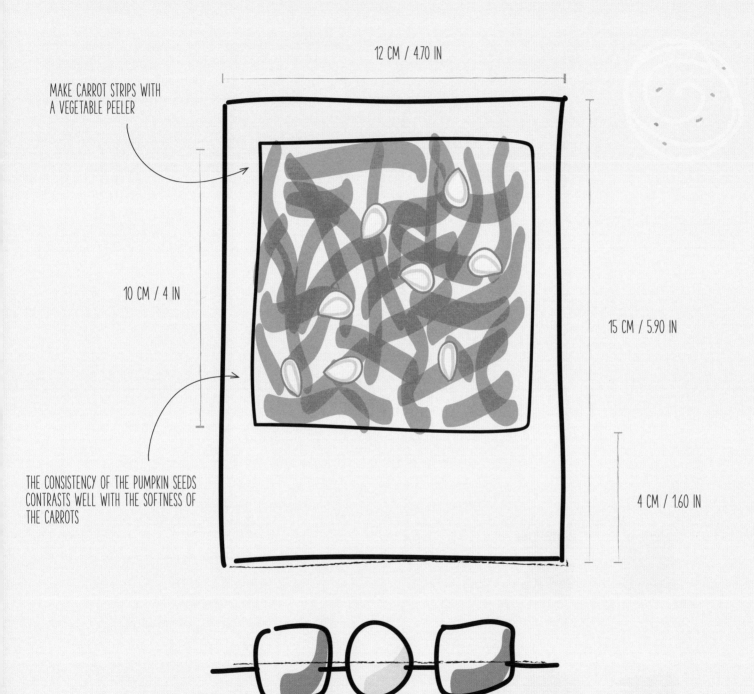

12 CM / 4.70 IN

MAKE CARROT STRIPS WITH
A VEGETABLE PEELER

10 CM / 4 IN

15 CM / 5.90 IN

THE CONSISTENCY OF THE PUMPKIN SEEDS
CONTRASTS WELL WITH THE SOFTNESS OF
THE CARROTS

4 CM / 1.60 IN

3 X 3 CM / 1.20 X 1.20 IN

PEACHES   MANGO

BRITTLE   GRAPES   APPLES

FRUIT SALAD AND SESAME BRITTLE

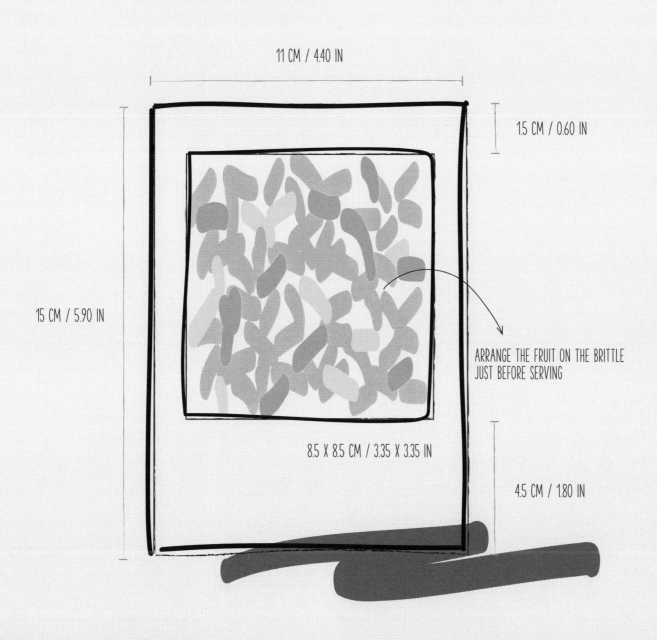

11 CM / 4.40 IN

1.5 CM / 0.60 IN

15 CM / 5.90 IN

ARRANGE THE FRUIT ON THE BRITTLE
JUST BEFORE SERVING

8.5 X 8.5 CM / 3.35 X 3.35 IN

4.5 CM / 1.80 IN

AS A FINAL TOUCH, DUST THE FRUIT WITH DEMERARA SUGAR
TO ADD SOME CRUNCH

CHICKEN TERIYAKI WITH BLACK BEANS

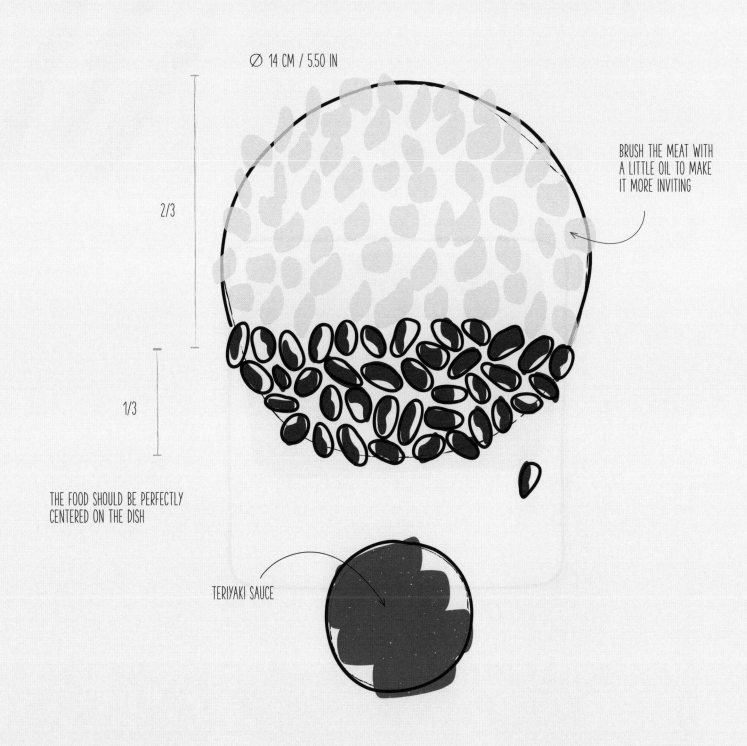

Ø 14 CM / 5.50 IN

2/3

1/3

BRUSH THE MEAT WITH
A LITTLE OIL TO MAKE
IT MORE INVITING

THE FOOD SHOULD BE PERFECTLY
CENTERED ON THE DISH

TERIYAKI SAUCE

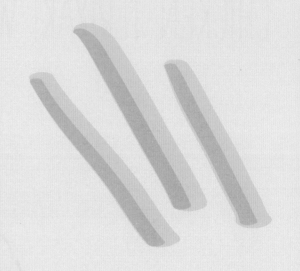

12 CM / 4.70 IN

12 CM / 4.70 IN

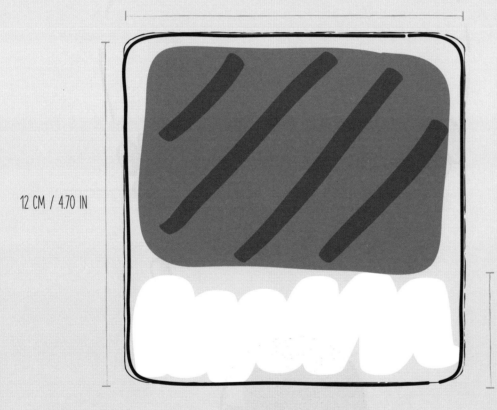

ARRANGE THE SAUCES USING A PASTRY BAG WITH
A MEDIUM TIP

3 CM / 1.20 IN

SQUARE BURGER WITH FRENCH FRIES

USE A PASTRY CUTTER TO
SHAPE THE HAMBURGER

12 CM / 4.70 IN

EDAM OR CHEDDAR CHEESE

12 CM / 4.70 IN

SERVE THE HAMBURGER OPEN-FACED
TO SHOW THE INGREDIENTS

KETCHUP

3 CM / 1.20 IN

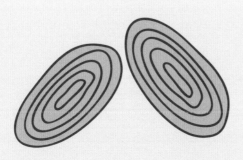

ROUND VEGETARIAN BURGER

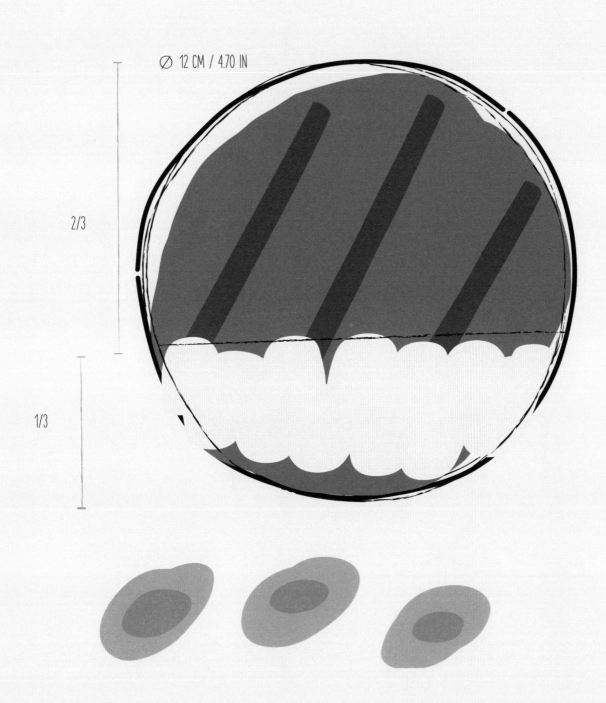

⌀ 12 CM / 4.70 IN

2/3

1/3

PISSALADIÈRE

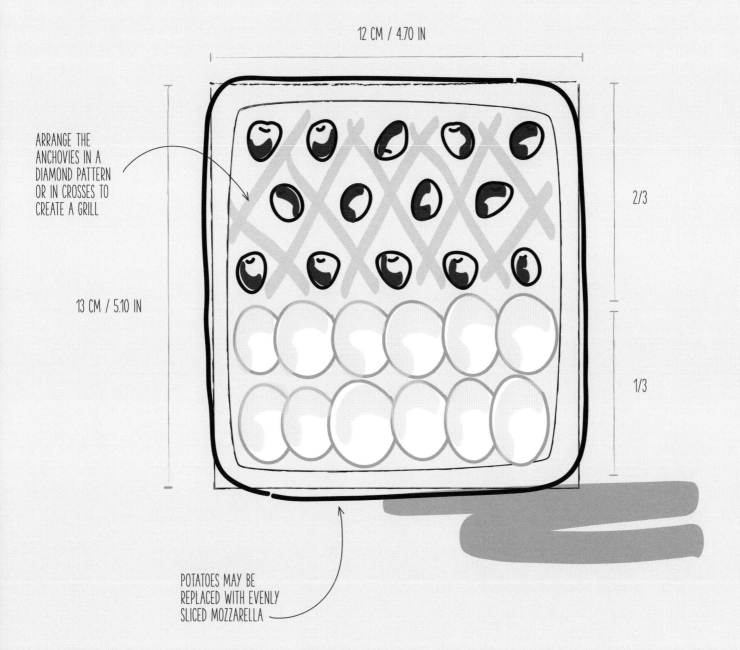

12 CM / 4.70 IN

13 CM / 5.10 IN

2/3

1/3

ARRANGE THE
ANCHOVIES IN A
DIAMOND PATTERN
OR IN CROSSES TO
CREATE A GRILL

POTATOES MAY BE
REPLACED WITH EVENLY
SLICED MOZZARELLA

COFFEE SEMIFREDDO

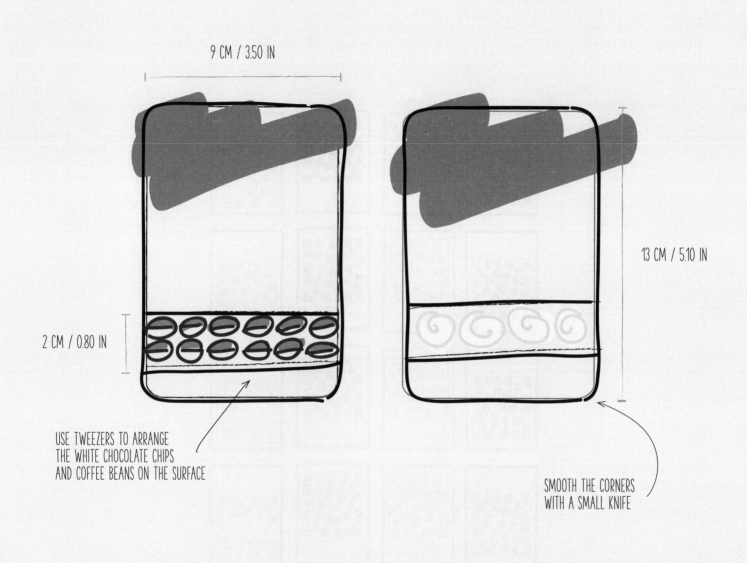

9 CM / 3.50 IN

13 CM / 5.10 IN

2 CM / 0.80 IN

USE TWEEZERS TO ARRANGE
THE WHITE CHOCOLATE CHIPS
AND COFFEE BEANS ON THE SURFACE

SMOOTH THE CORNERS
WITH A SMALL KNIFE

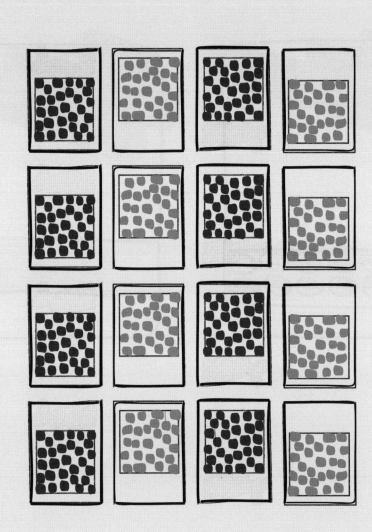

BROWNIES&WHITIES

TO CUT THE CHOCOLATE CUBES
EASILY, USE CHOCOLATE WITH A
LOWER PERCENTAGE OF COCOA

5 CM / 2 IN

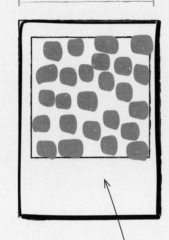

6.5 CM / 2.60 IN

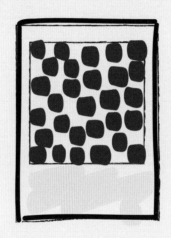

3 CM / 1.20 IN

THE TRANSPARENT CANDIED
FRUIT STANDS OUT ON THE
CRACKED SURFACE OF THE
BROWNIES

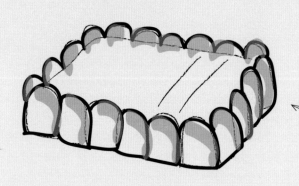

CREATE A "BAROQUE" FRAME
OF COOKIES THAT CONTRASTS
THE COMPOSITIONAL ESSENTIALITY
OF THE TIRAMISÙ

TIRAMISÙ

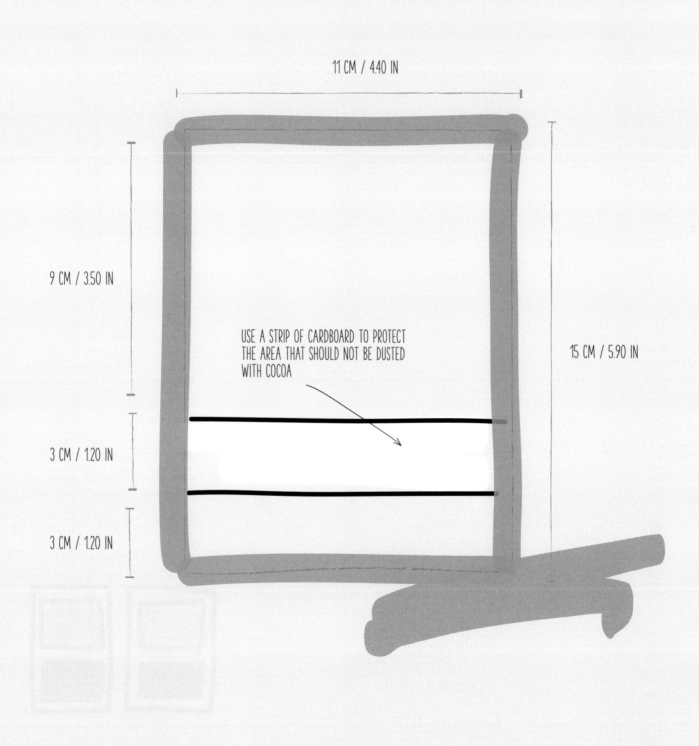

11 CM / 4.40 IN

9 CM / 3.50 IN

15 CM / 5.90 IN

USE A STRIP OF CARDBOARD TO PROTECT
THE AREA THAT SHOULD NOT BE DUSTED
WITH COCOA

3 CM / 1.20 IN

3 CM / 1.20 IN

SERVE THE CAKE WITH SQUARES
OF DECORATED CHOCOLATE. PAINT
THE CHOCOLATES WITH A LITTLE
HONEY OR JAM PRIOR TO SETTING
THE SUGAR ON THEM

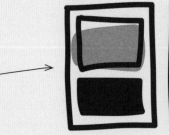

MOIST CHOCOLATE CAKE

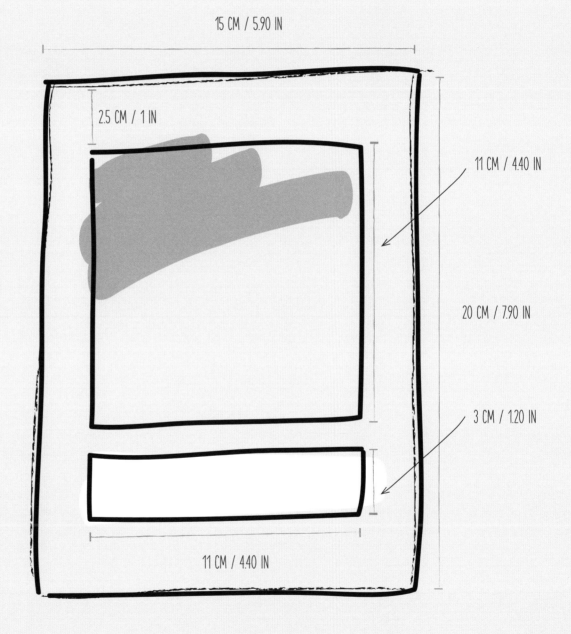

15 CM / 5.90 IN

2.5 CM / 1 IN

CREATE SURFACE
AREAS WITH
COLORED SUGAR
CRYSTALS, USING A
CARDBOARD STENCIL
TO PROTECT THE
AREAS THAT SHOULD
NOT BE DECORATED

11 CM / 4.40 IN

20 CM / 7.90 IN

3 CM / 1.20 IN

11 CM / 4.40 IN

USE A BRUSH TO CORRECT ANY
IMPERFECTIONS IN THE DECORATION

TOMATO ASPIC

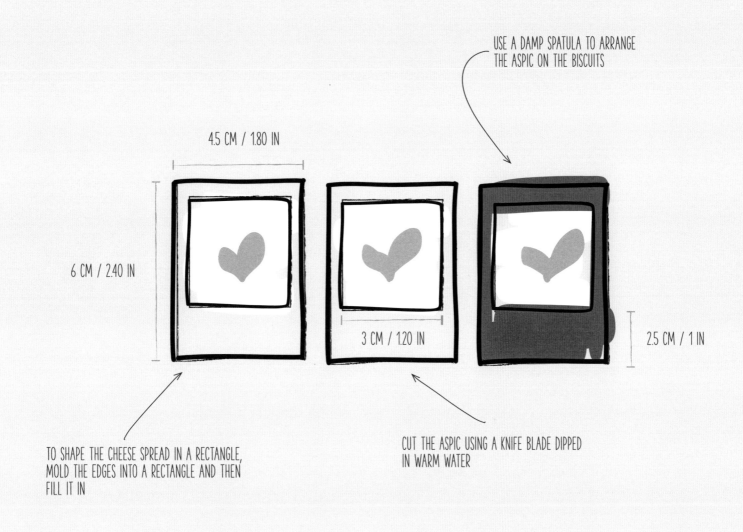

USE A DAMP SPATULA TO ARRANGE
THE ASPIC ON THE BISCUITS

4.5 CM / 1.80 IN

6 CM / 2.40 IN

3 CM / 1.20 IN

2.5 CM / 1 IN

TO SHAPE THE CHEESE SPREAD IN A RECTANGLE,
MOLD THE EDGES INTO A RECTANGLE AND THEN
FILL IT IN

CUT THE ASPIC USING A KNIFE BLADE DIPPED
IN WARM WATER

TERRINES

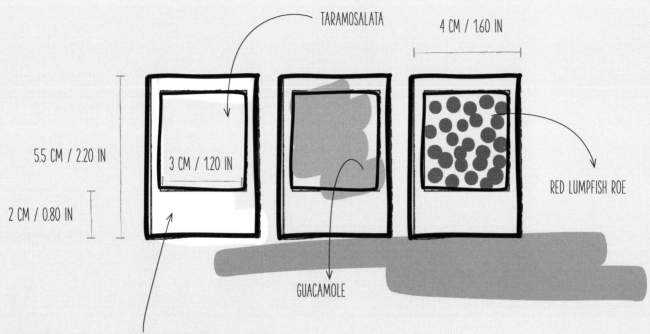

TARAMOSALATA

4 CM / 1.60 IN

5.5 CM / 2.20 IN

3 CM / 1.20 IN

2 CM / 0.80 IN

RED LUMPFISH ROE

GUACAMOLE

USE A STENCIL TECHNIQUE TO GARNISH THE TERRINES: CUT SQUARES
OUT OF THE SLICES OF BREAD USING A PASTRY CUTTER, CREATING A
FRAME; GARNISH THE SQUARES OF BREAD AND PUT THEM BACK IN
THE EMPTY FRAMES

THE TERRINES MAY BE ARRANGED IN AN ALTERNATING
PATTERN OR PRESENTED IN STRIPS OF RED TERRINES,
PINK TERRINES, GREEN TERRINES

CREATE A CHROMATIC RANGE:

RED TOMATO   YELLOW TOMATO

SQUARE PIZZA

DRESS THE TOMATOES AND MOZZARELLA AT THE LAST
MINUTE, WHEN THEY ARE ARRANGED, COLD, ON THE PIZZA

15 CM / 5.90 IN

15 CM / 5.90 IN

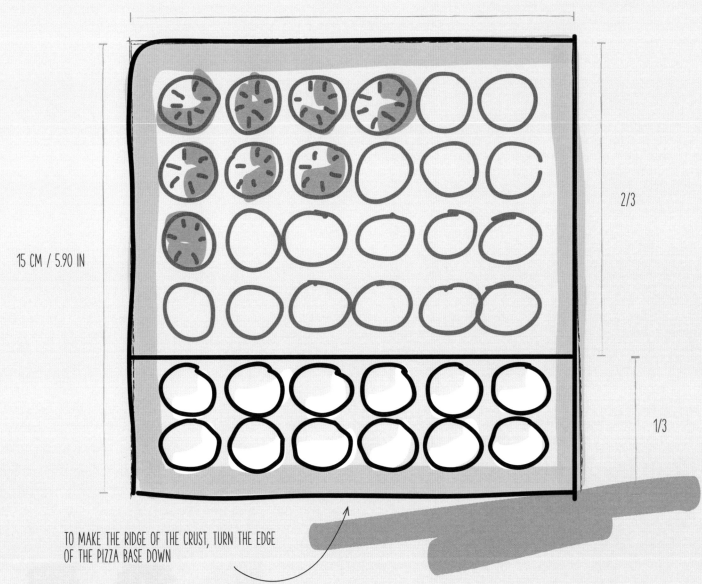

2/3

1/3

TO MAKE THE RIDGE OF THE CRUST, TURN THE EDGE
OF THE PIZZA BASE DOWN

BULGUR   POMEGRANATE   PISTACHIO

POMEGRANATE AND PISTACHIO BULGUR

TO SHAPE PRECISELY, USE THE STRAIGHT
BLADE OF A KNIFE OR DOUGH SCRAPER
AGAINST THE EDGE OF THE POMEGRANATE
AND ARRANGE THE PISTACHIOS

THE TOP AND BOTTOM OF THE
BULGUR SHOULD BE EQUALLY
COMPACT AND DENSE WITH
INGREDIENTS

13 CM / 5.10 IN

14 CM / 5.50 IN

4 CM / 1.60 IN

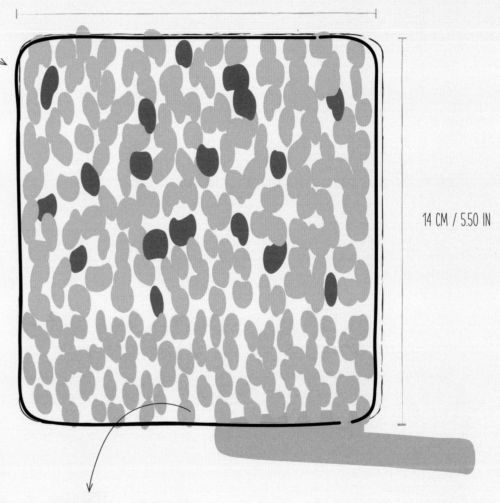

PARBOIL THE PISTACHIOS PRIOR TO PEELING

BREAD

TANDOORI
SAUCE

BASMATI
RICE

TANDOORI CHICKEN WITH BASMATI RICE

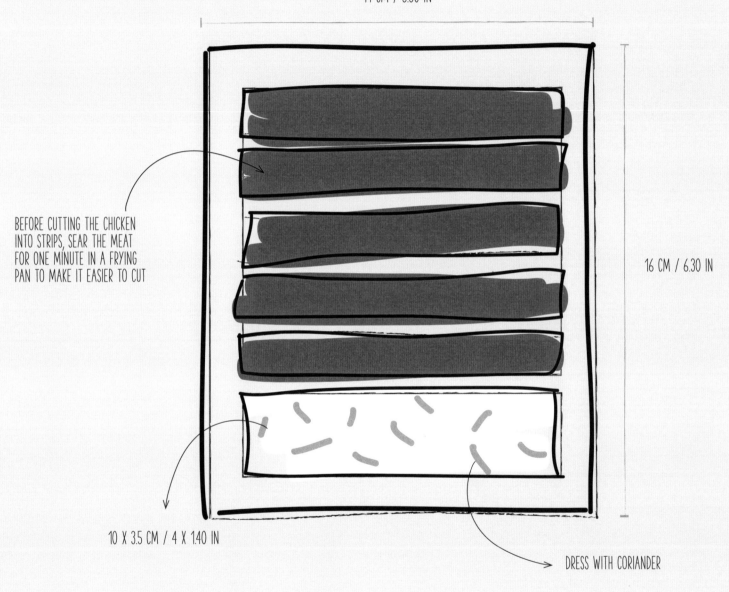

14 CM / 5.50 IN

16 CM / 6.30 IN

BEFORE CUTTING THE CHICKEN INTO STRIPS, SEAR THE MEAT FOR ONE MINUTE IN A FRYING PAN TO MAKE IT EASIER TO CUT

10 X 3.5 CM / 4 X 1.40 IN

DRESS WITH CORIANDER

ROUND MERINGUE WITH WILD STRAWBERRIES

Ø 15 CM / 5.90 IN

THE OVERFLOWING EFFECT
OF THE STRAWBERRIES
OFFSETS THE STIFFNESS
OF THE MERINGUES

2/3

1/3

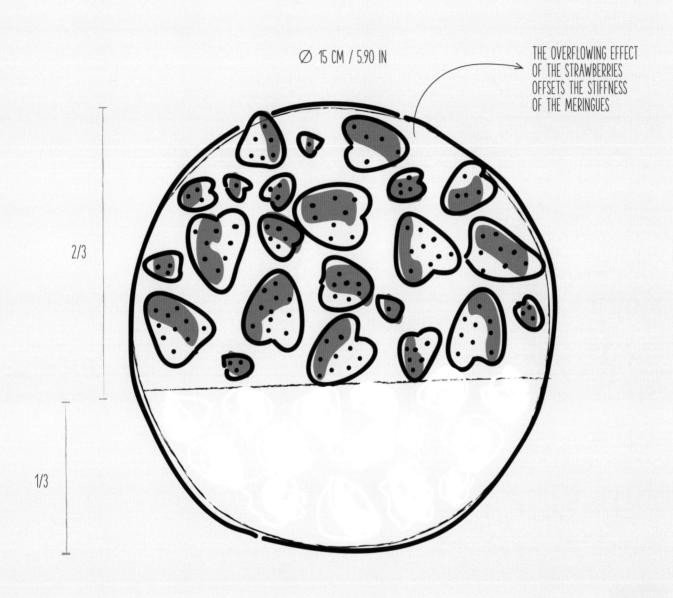

DRAW A CIRCLE WITH A PENCIL ON A PIECE OF BAKING PAPER TO
SHAPE THE TORTE. TURN THE PAPER OVER SO THE PENCIL MARKS
DON'T COME INTO CONTACT WITH THE INGREDIENTS

AVOCADO

 TUNA

TUNA TARTARE AND GUACAMOLE

ARRANGE THE PLATTER JUST BEFORE SERVING
SO THE CRUST DOES NOT GET SOGGY

12 CM / 4.70 IN

3/4

1/4

COOL THE TUNA IN THE FREEZER
BEFORE CUTTING IT INTO CUBES:
THE FLESH WILL BE MORE COMPACT
AND THE CUT MORE PRECISE

TRIANGULAR CHIPS LIGHTEN
THE COMPOSITION

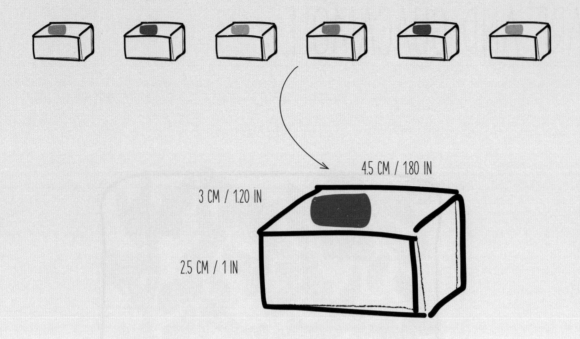

4.5 CM / 1.80 IN

3 CM / 1.20 IN

2.5 CM / 1 IN

NIGIRI SET

TUNA

SALMON

GREEN TOBIKO

RED TOBIKO

RED LUMPFISH ROE

ORANGE TOBIKO

ARRANGE THE NIGIRI IN A
GEOMETRIC COMPOSITION

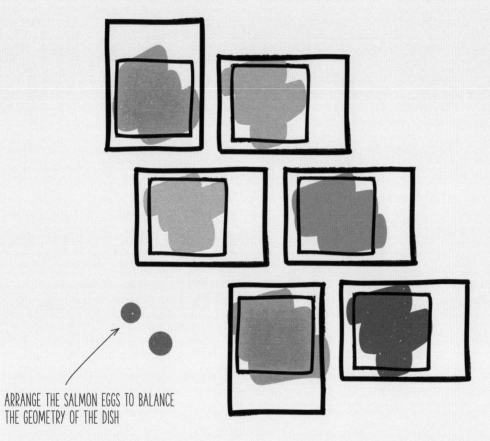

ARRANGE THE SALMON EGGS TO BALANCE
THE GEOMETRY OF THE DISH

3 CM / 1.20 IN

BROWN THE TOFU IN A FRYING PAN
TO MAKE IT SLIGHTLY CRISPY

5 CM / 2 IN

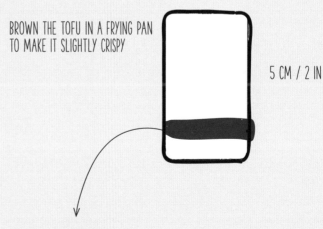

STRIP OF NORI SEAWEED

SEARED SALMON WITH VENERE RICE

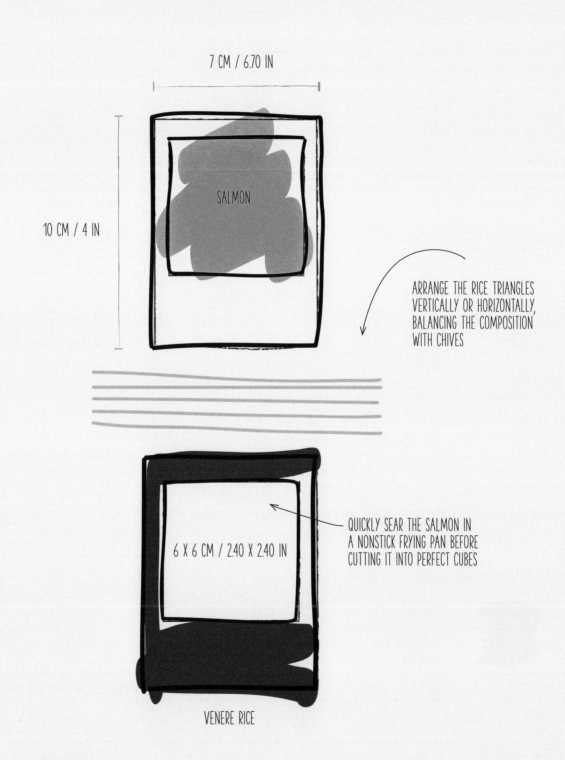

7 CM / 6.70 IN

10 CM / 4 IN

SALMON

ARRANGE THE RICE TRIANGLES
VERTICALLY OR HORIZONTALLY,
BALANCING THE COMPOSITION
WITH CHIVES

6 X 6 CM / 2.40 X 2.40 IN

QUICKLY SEAR THE SALMON IN
A NONSTICK FRYING PAN BEFORE
CUTTING IT INTO PERFECT CUBES

VENERE RICE

POMEGRANATE

ROSE PETALS

SEA BREAM

HORSERADISH

SEA BREAM TARTARE WITH ROSE PETALS

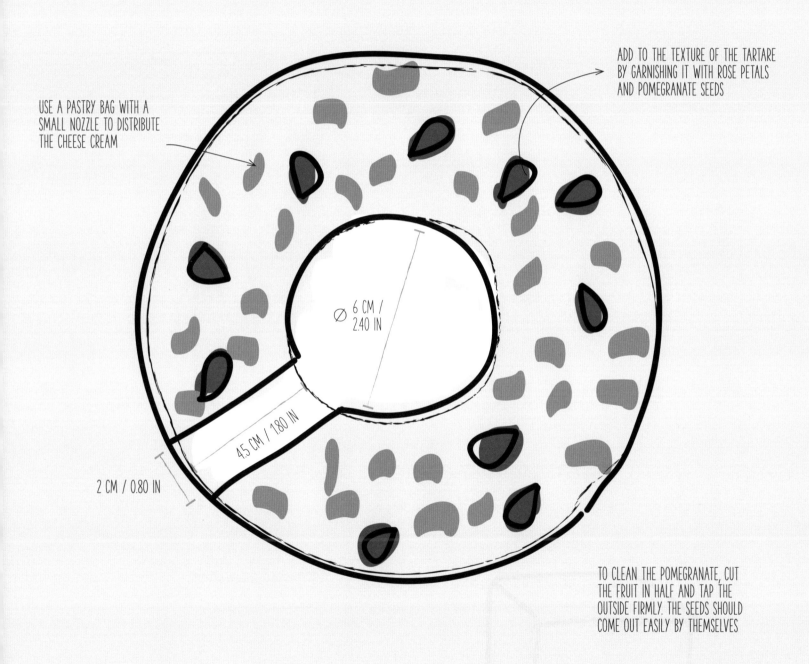

USE A PASTRY BAG WITH A SMALL NOZZLE TO DISTRIBUTE THE CHEESE CREAM

ADD TO THE TEXTURE OF THE TARTARE BY GARNISHING IT WITH ROSE PETALS AND POMEGRANATE SEEDS

Ø 6 CM / 2.40 IN

4.5 CM / 1.80 IN

2 CM / 0.80 IN

TO CLEAN THE POMEGRANATE, CUT THE FRUIT IN HALF AND TAP THE OUTSIDE FIRMLY. THE SEEDS SHOULD COME OUT EASILY BY THEMSELVES

4 CM / 1.60 IN

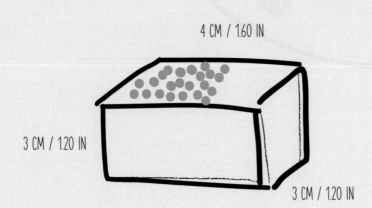

3 CM / 1.20 IN

3 CM / 1.20 IN

CAKESICLES

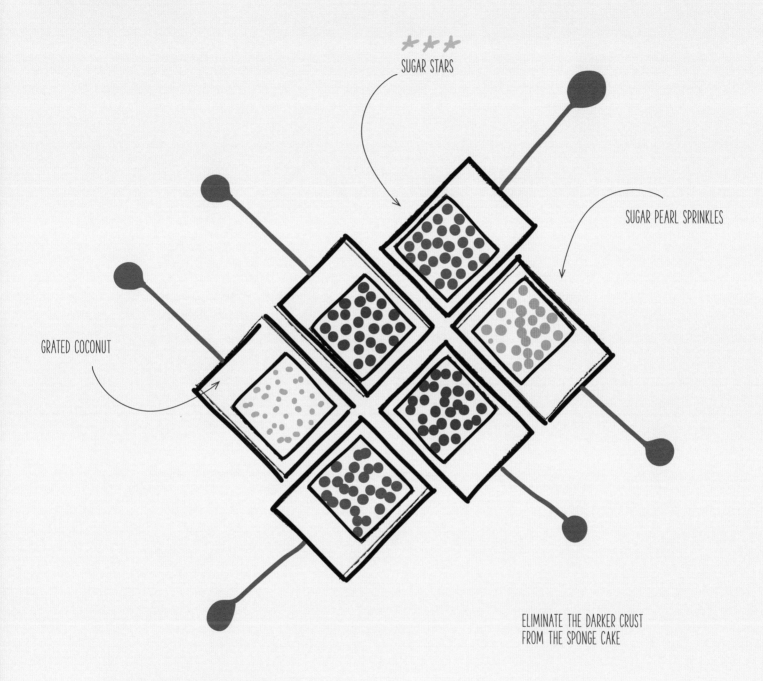

SUGAR STARS

SUGAR PEARL SPRINKLES

GRATED COCONUT

ELIMINATE THE DARKER CRUST
FROM THE SPONGE CAKE

PUT THE CAKE POP MIXTURE IN THE FREEZER TO
HARDEN IT AND MAKE IT EASIER TO WORK WITH

THREESECAKE

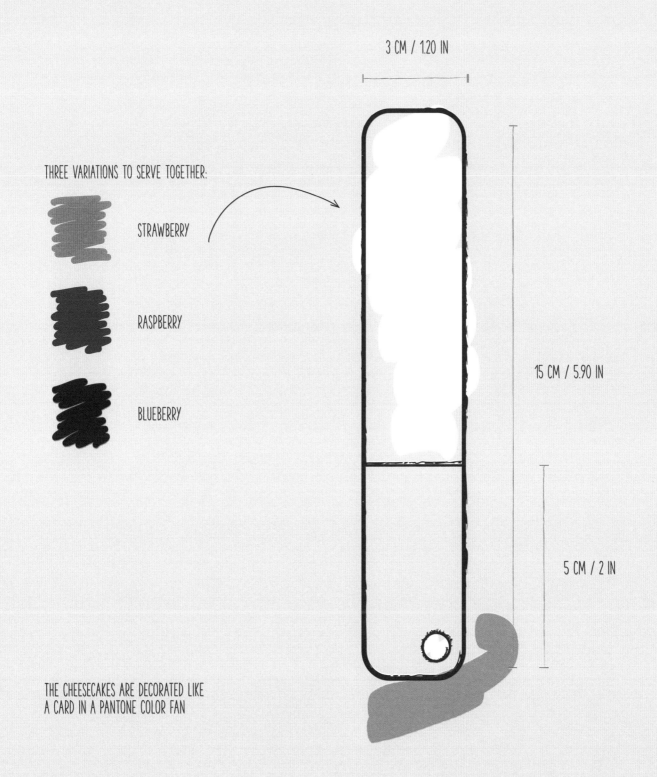

THREE VARIATIONS TO SERVE TOGETHER:

STRAWBERRY

RASPBERRY

BLUEBERRY

THE CHEESECAKES ARE DECORATED LIKE
A CARD IN A PANTONE COLOR FAN

3 CM / 1.20 IN

15 CM / 5.90 IN

5 CM / 2 IN

CABBAGE WITH CHICKPEAS DUMPLINGS

A GEOMETRIC COMPOSITION THAT COMBINES
SQUARE AND ROUND SHAPES

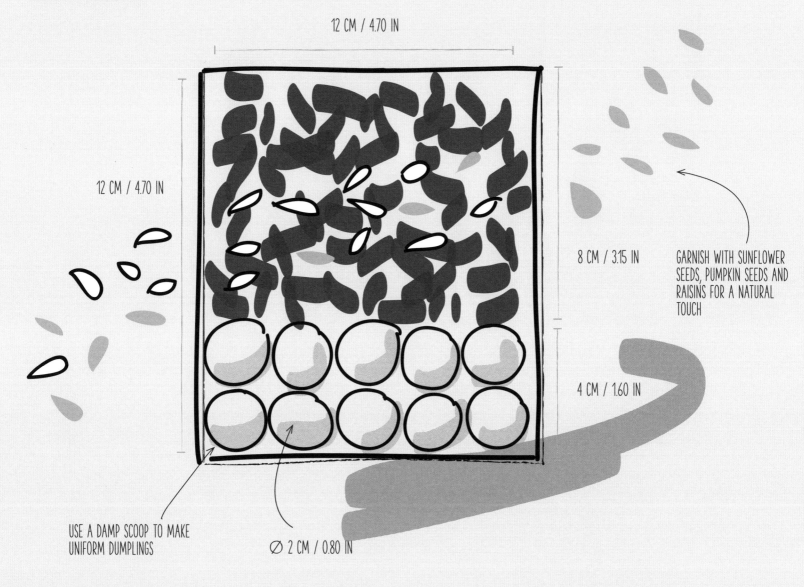

12 CM / 4.70 IN

12 CM / 4.70 IN

8 CM / 3.15 IN

GARNISH WITH SUNFLOWER
SEEDS, PUMPKIN SEEDS AND
RAISINS FOR A NATURAL
TOUCH

4 CM / 1.60 IN

USE A DAMP SCOOP TO MAKE
UNIFORM DUMPLINGS

Ø 2 CM / 0.80 IN

BEET AND PUMPKIN RAVIOLI

ALIGN THE RAVIOLI TO CREATE
A VERY STYLIZED PRESENTATION

ADD SAFFRON TO THE FILLING TO OBTAIN
A VERY BRIGHT ORANGE COLOR

4 CM / 1.60 IN

4 CM / 1.60 IN

OCTOPUS SALAD WITH PURPLE PUREE

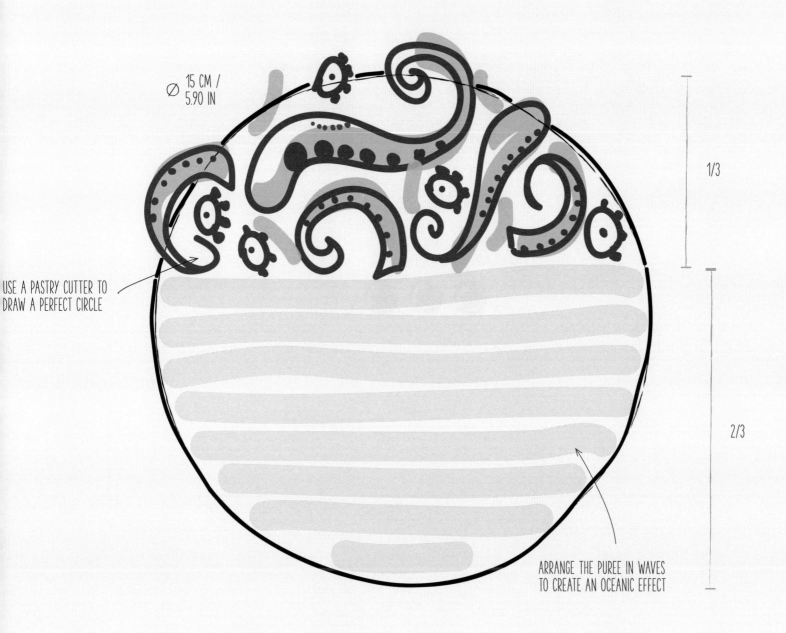

⌀ 15 CM /
5.90 IN

1/3

2/3

USE A PASTRY CUTTER TO
DRAW A PERFECT CIRCLE

ARRANGE THE PUREE IN WAVES
TO CREATE AN OCEANIC EFFECT

THE DISH SHOULD BE SIMPLE,
BUT CAREFULLY DETAILED

FRESH CURRANTS MAY BE ADDED TO MAKE
THE COLOR RANGE MORE VIBRANT AND
LEND TARTNESS TO THE FLAVOR

FOX GRAPE PUDDING

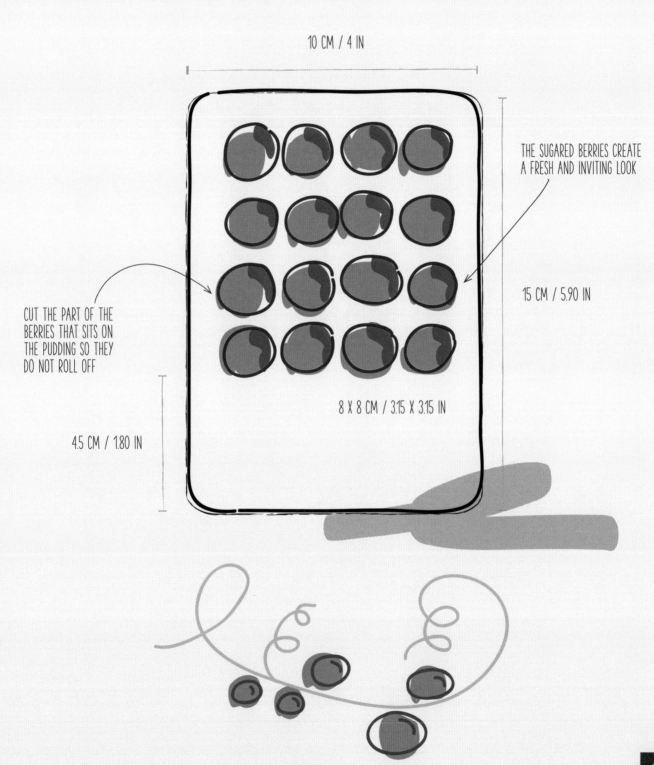

10 CM / 4 IN

THE SUGARED BERRIES CREATE
A FRESH AND INVITING LOOK

15 CM / 5.90 IN

CUT THE PART OF THE
BERRIES THAT SITS ON
THE PUDDING SO THEY
DO NOT ROLL OFF

8 X 8 CM / 3.15 X 3.15 IN

4.5 CM / 1.80 IN

BLUEBERRY CHEESECAKE

16 CM / 6.30 IN

16 CM / 6.30 IN

ARRANGE THE BLUEBERRIES IN CLOSE, EVEN ROWS

3 CM / 1.20 IN

1 CM / 0.40 IN

THE CAKE EDGE OF THE TART SHOULD BE COMPACT AND SQUARE TO FRAME THE CREAM AND BLUEBERRIES

SALAD WITH BORAGE FLOWERS

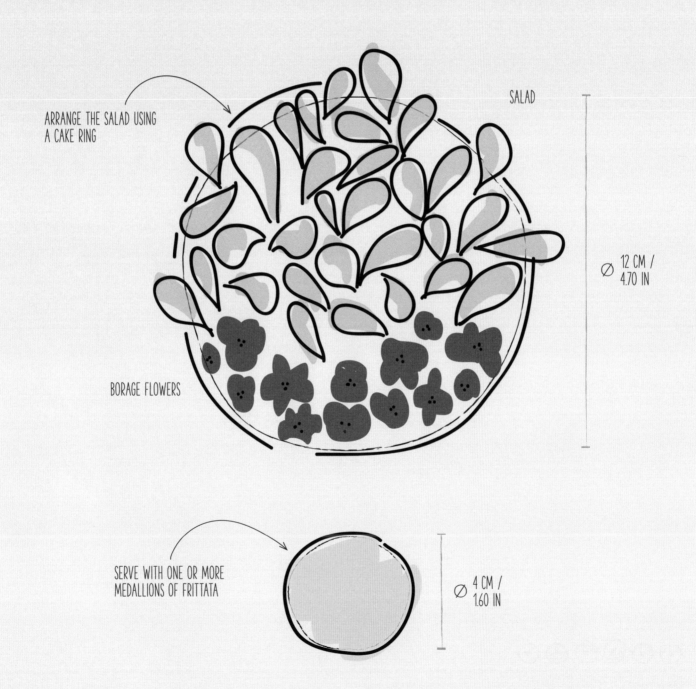

ARRANGE THE SALAD USING
A CAKE RING

SALAD

Ø 12 CM /
4.70 IN

BORAGE FLOWERS

SERVE WITH ONE OR MORE
MEDALLIONS OF FRITTATA

Ø 4 CM /
1.60 IN

FOR TON-SUR-TON EFFECT, BLUEBERRIES
CAN BE USED TO SUBSTITUTE THE APPLE

BLUE CABBAGE RISOTTO AND GREEN APPLE

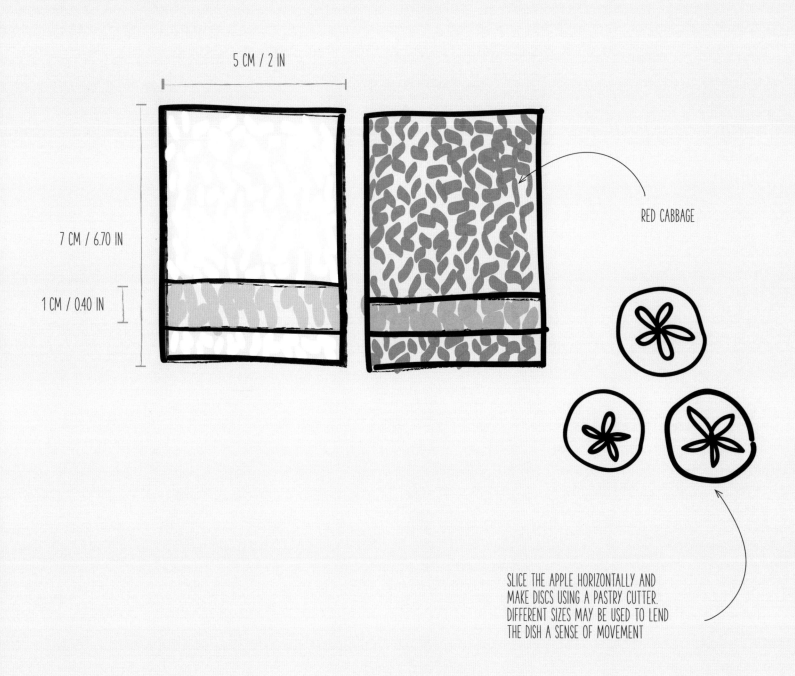

5 CM / 2 IN

7 CM / 6.70 IN

1 CM / 0.40 IN

RED CABBAGE

SLICE THE APPLE HORIZONTALLY AND
MAKE DISCS USING A PASTRY CUTTER.
DIFFERENT SIZES MAY BE USED TO LEND
THE DISH A SENSE OF MOVEMENT

SABLÉ TART WITH ANCHOVIES

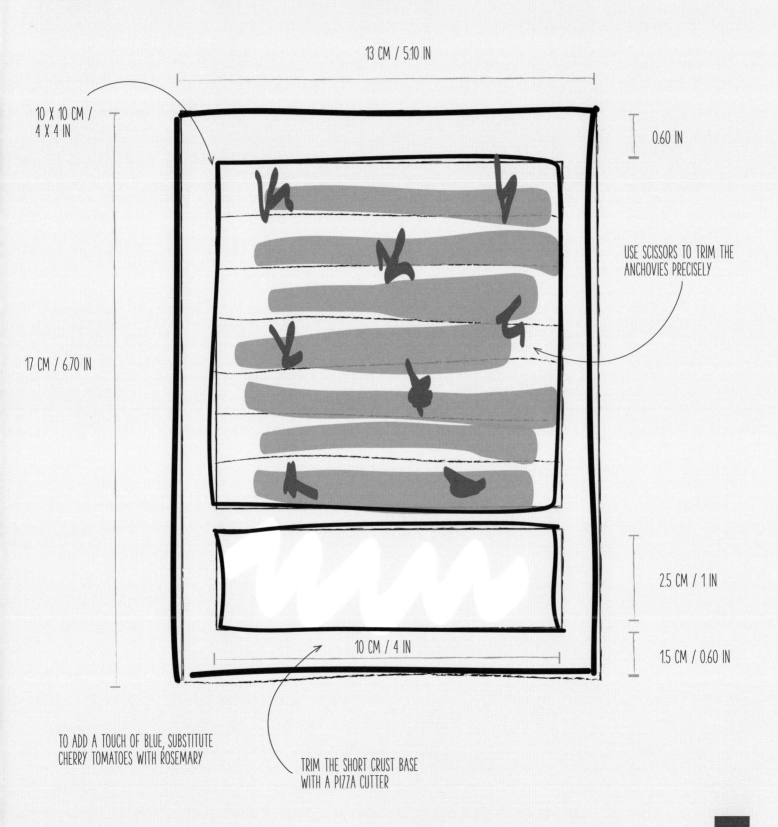

13 CM / 5.10 IN

10 X 10 CM / 4 X 4 IN

0.60 IN

17 CM / 6.70 IN

USE SCISSORS TO TRIM THE ANCHOVIES PRECISELY

2.5 CM / 1 IN

10 CM / 4 IN

1.5 CM / 0.60 IN

TO ADD A TOUCH OF BLUE, SUBSTITUTE CHERRY TOMATOES WITH ROSEMARY

TRIM THE SHORT CRUST BASE WITH A PIZZA CUTTER

BLUEBIRD AND ROBIN BISCUITS

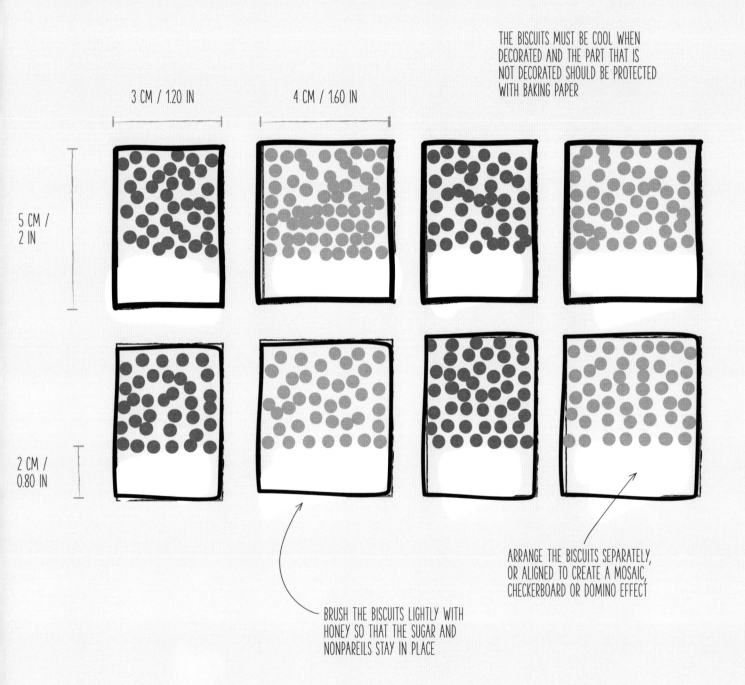

3 CM / 1.20 IN

4 CM / 1.60 IN

THE BISCUITS MUST BE COOL WHEN DECORATED AND THE PART THAT IS NOT DECORATED SHOULD BE PROTECTED WITH BAKING PAPER

5 CM / 2 IN

2 CM / 0.80 IN

BRUSH THE BISCUITS LIGHTLY WITH HONEY SO THAT THE SUGAR AND NONPAREILS STAY IN PLACE

ARRANGE THE BISCUITS SEPARATELY, OR ALIGNED TO CREATE A MOSAIC, CHECKERBOARD OR DOMINO EFFECT

DONUTS

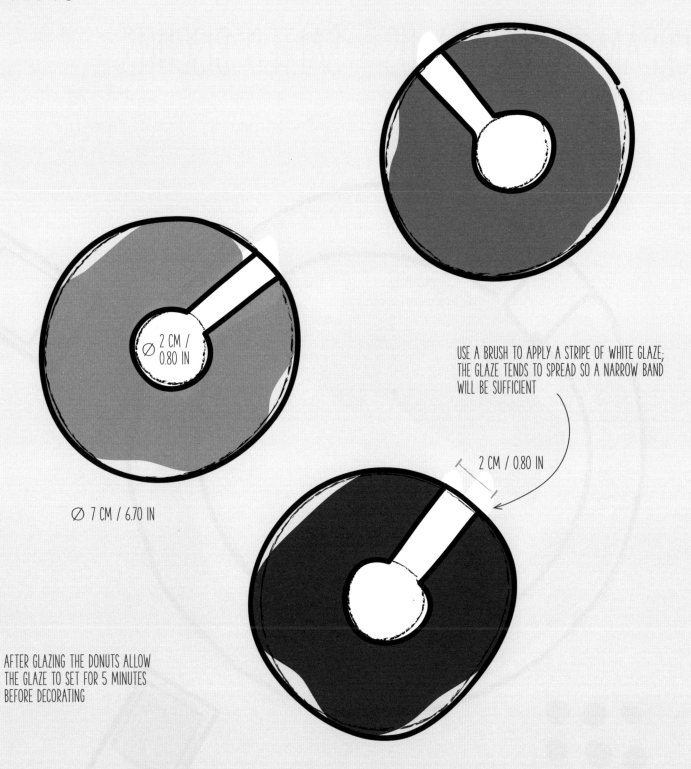

⌀ 2 CM / 0.80 IN

⌀ 7 CM / 6.70 IN

USE A BRUSH TO APPLY A STRIPE OF WHITE GLAZE; THE GLAZE TENDS TO SPREAD SO A NARROW BAND WILL BE SUFFICIENT

2 CM / 0.80 IN

AFTER GLAZING THE DONUTS ALLOW THE GLAZE TO SET FOR 5 MINUTES BEFORE DECORATING

PUREED SPINACH + CREAMED PEAS
CREAM OF ASPARAGUS + SALTED BISCUITS

MEZZAMANICA · CAULIFLOWER · BROCCOLI · RICOTTA

MEZZEMANICHE WITH BROCCOLI AND RICOTTA

14 CM / 5.50 IN

14 CM / 5.50 IN

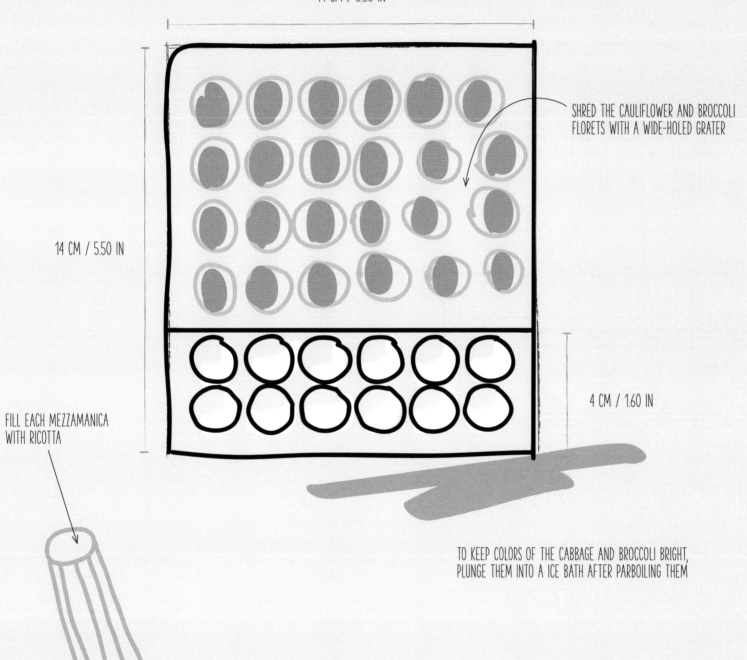

SHRED THE CAULIFLOWER AND BROCCOLI
FLORETS WITH A WIDE-HOLED GRATER

4 CM / 1.60 IN

FILL EACH MEZZAMANICA
WITH RICOTTA

TO KEEP COLORS OF THE CABBAGE AND BROCCOLI BRIGHT,
PLUNGE THEM INTO A ICE BATH AFTER PARBOILING THEM

PORK LOIN WITH SESAME SEEDS

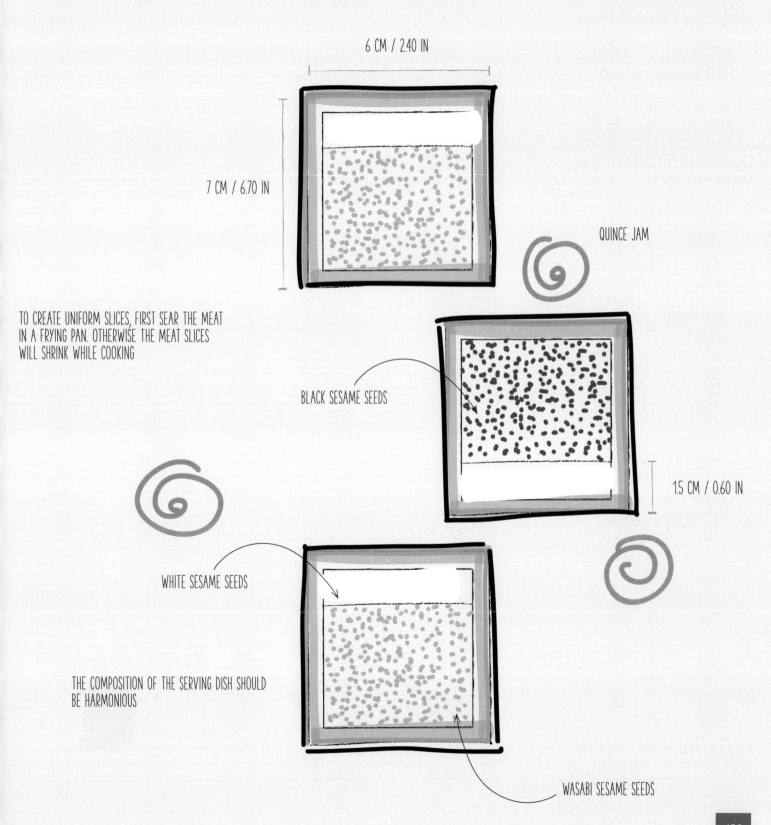

6 CM / 2.40 IN

7 CM / 6.70 IN

QUINCE JAM

TO CREATE UNIFORM SLICES, FIRST SEAR THE MEAT IN A FRYING PAN. OTHERWISE THE MEAT SLICES WILL SHRINK WHILE COOKING

BLACK SESAME SEEDS

1.5 CM / 0.60 IN

WHITE SESAME SEEDS

THE COMPOSITION OF THE SERVING DISH SHOULD BE HARMONIOUS

WASABI SESAME SEEDS

PUFF PASTRY + BÉCHAMEL + CHEESE + ASPARAGUS

SAVORY ASPARAGUS TARTS

12 CM / 4.70 IN

TO KEEP THE ASPARAGUS BRIGHT GREEN,
PLUNGE SHOOTS INTO ICE WATER FOR
2 MINUTES AFTER PARBOILING

DUST THE STRIP OF CHEESE WITH PEPPER
TO MAKE THE SURFACE LESS UNIFORM

17 CM / 6.70 IN

3 CM / 1.20 IN

SPINACH AND PINE NUT LONG CAKE

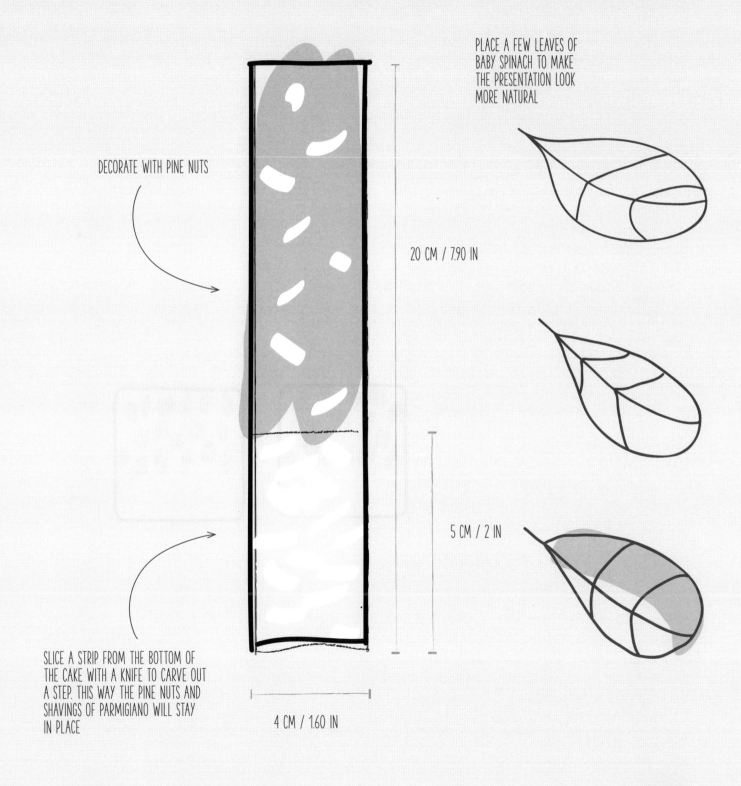

DECORATE WITH PINE NUTS

PLACE A FEW LEAVES OF BABY SPINACH TO MAKE THE PRESENTATION LOOK MORE NATURAL

20 CM / 7.90 IN

5 CM / 2 IN

SLICE A STRIP FROM THE BOTTOM OF THE CAKE WITH A KNIFE TO CARVE OUT A STEP. THIS WAY THE PINE NUTS AND SHAVINGS OF PARMIGIANO WILL STAY IN PLACE

4 CM / 1.60 IN

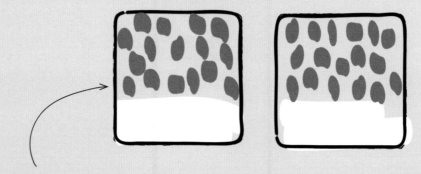

YOU CAN USE WALNUTS INSTEAD OF PISTACHIOS

PISTACHIO GREEN CAKES

THE CAKES SHOULD BE ARRANGED
SIDE BY SIDE ON A SERVING DISH
AS FINGER FOOD

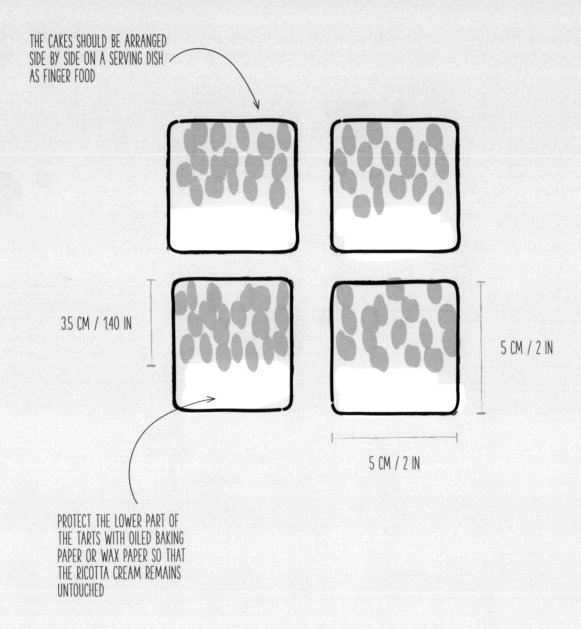

3.5 CM / 1.40 IN

5 CM / 2 IN

5 CM / 2 IN

PROTECT THE LOWER PART OF
THE TARTS WITH OILED BAKING
PAPER OR WAX PAPER SO THAT
THE RICOTTA CREAM REMAINS
UNTOUCHED

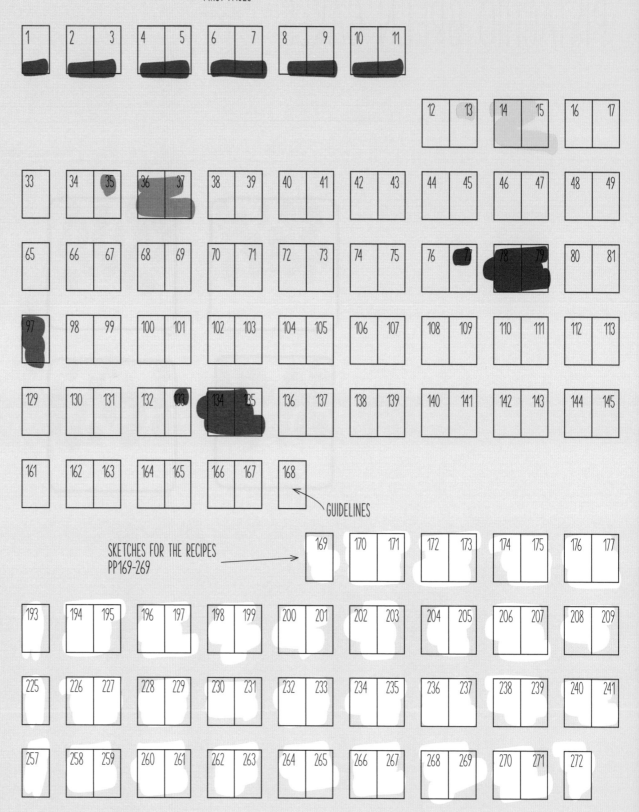

FIRST PAGES

1

2 3

4 5

6 7

8 9

10 11

12 13

14 15

16 17

33

34 35

36 37

38 39

40 41

42 43

44 45

46 47

48 49

65

66 67

68 69

70 71

72 73

74 75

76 77

78 79

80 81

97

98 99

100 101

102 103

104 105

106 107

108 109

110 111

112 113

129

130 131

132 133

134 135

136 137

138 139

140 141

142 143

144 145

161

162 163

164 165

166 167

168

GUIDELINES

SKETCHES FOR THE RECIPES
PP169-269

169

170 171

172 173

174 175

176 177

193

194 195

196 197

198 199

200 201

202 203

204 205

206 207

208 209

225

226 227

228 229

230 231

232 233

234 235

236 237

238 239

240 241

257

258 259

260 261

262 263

264 265

266 267

268 269

270 271

272

273

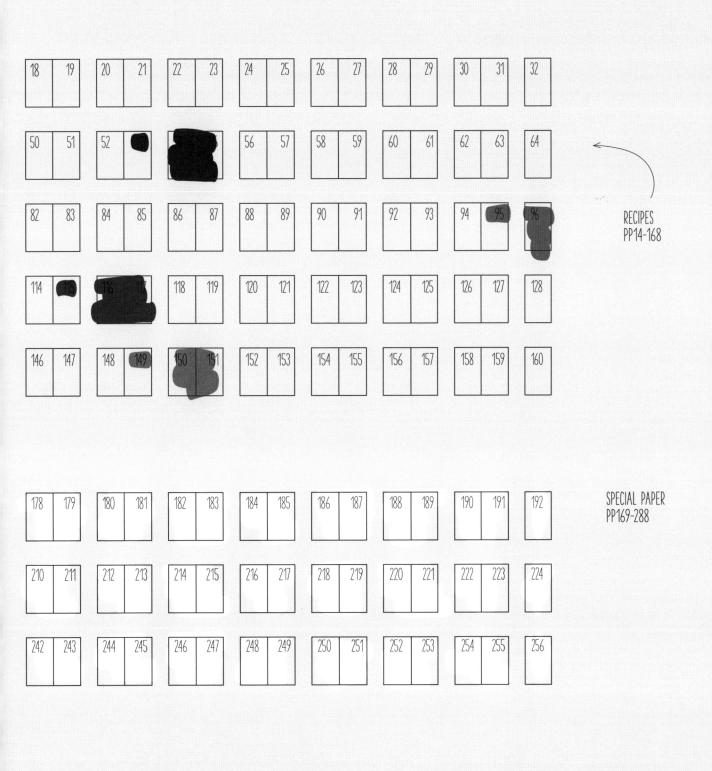

18 19	20 21	22 23	24 25	26 27	28 29	30 31	32		
50 51	52		56 57	58 59	60 61	62 63	64		
82 83	84 85	86 87	88 89	90 91	92 93	94 95	96		
114 115	116 117	118 119	120 121	122 123	124 125	126 127	128		
146 147	148 149	150 151	152 153	154 155	156 157	158 159	160		

RECIPES
PP14-168

178 179	180 181	182 183	184 185	186 187	188 189	190 191	192	
210 211	212 213	214 215	216 217	218 219	220 221	222 223	224	
242 243	244 245	246 247	248 249	250 251	252 253	254 255	256	

SPECIAL PAPER
PP169-288

274 275	276 277	278 279	280 281	282 283	284 285	286 287	288

CHECKLIST & MENU

checklist

- [ ] adjustable molds (round and square/rectangular)
- [ ] baking paper
- [ ] baking sheet
- [ ] bowls
- [ ] cake ring with handles
- [ ] cardboard
- [ ] ceramic pie weights

- [ ] cheesecloth
- [ ] chopping board
- [ ] cooling rack
- [ ] deep fryer
- [ ] digital thermometer
- [ ] disposable aluminum baking pan
- [ ] electric beater with dough hook and beaters

- [ ] electronic scale
- [ ] floral foam base or polystyrene former
- [ ] food processor
- [ ] frying pan with basket
- [ ] grater
- [ ] hand whisk
- [ ] immersion blender

- [ ] jug blender
- [ ] juicer
- [ ] kitchen paper
- [ ] knives
- [ ] long zester
- [ ] mandoline
- [ ] measuring spoons
- [ ] melon baller
- [ ] metal sheet
- [ ] mortar and pestle
- [ ] non-stick board and mat
- [ ] pastry bag and tips with different shapes and sizes

- [ ] pastry cutter (round, rectangular, square...) in different sizes
- [ ] pastry wheel
- [ ] plastic wrap
- [ ] potato masher
- [ ] rolling pin
- [ ] scrapers
- [ ] set of brushes of different sizes
- [ ] sheets of gelatin
- [ ] sieve and colander
- [ ] silicone brushes
- [ ] skimmer and spiral spider strainer
- [ ] spatulas in different kinds of materials

- [ ] squeezer bottle in polyethylene
- [ ] stainless steel cheese slicer
- [ ] stainless steel dough roller
- [ ] stainless steel expandable frame and cutter
- [ ] stand mixer with dough hook and beaters
- [ ] steel steamer basket
- [ ] tongs and tweezers
- [ ] toothpicks
- [ ] vegetable peeler
- [ ] wok
- [ ] wooden spoon
- [ ] wooden sticks

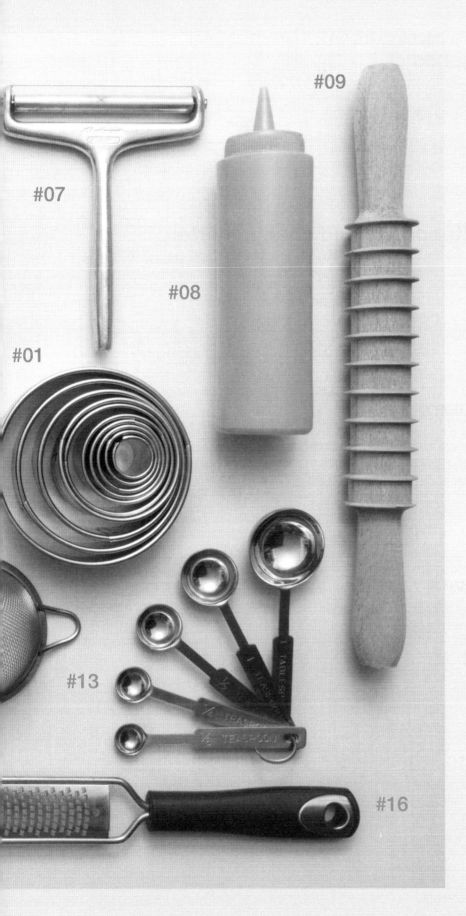

#09

#07

#08

#01

#13

#16

#01 pastry cutter

#02 pastry bag tips

#03 tweezers

#04 tongs

#05 brushes

#06 butter cutter

#07 cheese cutter

#08 squeezer bottle

#09 pasta rolling pin

#10 knives

#11 hand whisk

#12 sieve

#13 measuring spoons

#14 vegetable peeler

#15 ruler

#16 long zester

pastry cutter #01

A basic tool, pastry cutters are available in a variety of shapes (round, square, rectangular…), materials (the best are made of stainless steel) and in many sizes, even adjustable. In this cookbook they are used to cut the bases for our recipes, and even to arrange servings on a dish. If you do not have the right size, you can also make a temporary one from lightweight cardboard to help create the desired shape.

pastry bag tips #02

A set of tips is a necessary tool in the kitchen—along with a professional reusable pastry bag made of nylon or a single-use bag made of polyethylene—of any aspiring food stylist.

tongs and tweezers #03 #04

Some say perfection is impossible, but in order to come close when arranging dishes to serve… tongs and tweezers are a must. Long, short, stainless steel, plastic, pointed or wide, they are all very useful for positioning ingredients large or small.

brushes #05

A couple of long brushes (flat tipped and round) can be useful on a variety of occasions: to make a leaf shiny, to spread a thin glaze of honey on shortbread cookies, to glaze donuts…

butter cutter and cheese cutter #06 #07

Our grandmothers used these vintage kitchen tools to cut flavored butter and cheddar cheese. They may also be used to cut mozzarella and semi-hard cheeses such as Edam.

squeezer bottle #08

Made of polyethylene (flexible and resistant, dishwasher safe), a squeezer bottle may be used for sauces and seasonings. In this cookbook it is used for emulsifying and pouring citronette dressing for salad with borage flowers, and to distribute ketchup and mustard to serve with hamburgers.

knives #10

"Only a few, but very good" was once the rule in kitchens and never has it been truer than for knives. Choose whichever knives you like (steel, ceramic, nonstick coating…) but be sure the blades are well sharpened to ensure a clean and precise cut.

hand whisk #11

The classic steel hand whisk is fine, but if you need to buy one, choose a plastic or silicone-coated whisk: they are perfect for liquids and semi-dense mixtures and may be used in non-stick pans (including frying pans) since they are heat resistant.

sieve #12

Whether you call it a strainer, drainer or pointy-ended chinois, there is at least one in every house. You can use an especially fine sieve to strain liquids, too. If yours does not have fine holes, use a piece of gauze to increase its filtering "powers."

measuring spoons #13

Our measuring spoons show the American measures on one side (tablespoon and teaspoon) and milliliters on the other. 1 tablespoon corresponds to 15 milliliters, 1 teaspoon to 5 milliliters, and so on.

vegetable peeler #14

To remove the skin from a variety of fruits and vegetables as well as to peel away the fibrous part of particularly tough asparagus.

ruler #15

Your quest for precision should not become obsessive, but a ruler can always help set things a little straighter!

long zester #16

A must in every kitchen, used to finely grate any type of food, from lemons and oranges to chocolate and cheeses…

these will come in handy too...

cooling rack

A grid-patterned wire rack is ideal for cooling oven-baked preparations (prevents the base from getting damp) and draining excess glaze from donuts and cakes. If you need to buy a brand new rack, choose one coated with a nonstick finish, you won't regret it!

flour sifter

There are several different kinds, made of various materials and in a variety of sizes, a sieve is useful for any preparation involving flour or starch. Use it to sift any powdery ingredients and prevent lumping.

mandoline

Among the different models available on the market, avoid those made of plastic with a metal blade. Choose a professional-grade mandoline with "legs," a comfortable hand guard snaps and a gripper (keep your fingers safe!), to cut both slices and julienne.

spatula

Long, non-perforated spatulas (L-shaped spatulas are best) in stainless steel, flexible nylon or silicone are perfect for spreading cream and glazes and leveling out batter in pans. Silicone ones make it possible to scrape mixing bowls, blenders and food processors clean. Wide, angled-surface cake lifters are most useful for moving delicate bases without damage, flip and serve frittatas to a dish or move diced vegetables into the pan.

menu

#glutton

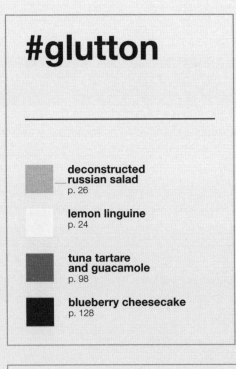

deconstructed
russian salad
p. 26

lemon linguine
p. 24

tuna tartare
and guacamole
p. 98

blueberry cheesecake
p. 128

#light

pureed spinach+creamed
peas
p. 154

salad with borage flowers
p. 136

pork loin
with sesame seeds
p. 158

fox grape pudding
p. 126

#veg

rye bread appetizers
p. 16

mezzemaniche
with broccoli and ricotta
p. 156

frittata with radicchio
& walnut salad
p. 42

pistachio green cakes
p. 164

#serenity rose

salad with borage flowers
p. 136

blue cabbage risotto
and green apple
p. 138

sea bream tartare
with rose petals
p. 106

#brunch

#tasty

#salty party

#earth

#tex-mex

#fusion

#spring

 savory asparagus tarts
p. 160

 cream of asparagus + salted biscuits
p. 155

 salad with borage flowers
p. 136

 tarte citron
p. 30

#healthy

 pureed spinach+creamed peas
p. 154

 red mullet on sweet potato
p. 44

 cabbage with chickpeas dumplings
p. 118

 fruit salad and sesame brittle
p. 48

#friends

 tomato aspic
p. 80

 blue cabbage risotto and green apple
p. 138

 carrot salad with kefta
p. 46

 tiramisù
p. 70

#5o'clock tea

 bluebird and robin biscuits
p. 142

 brownies&whities
p. 68

#japan time

 nigiri set
p. 100

 chicken teriyaki with black beans
p. 56

#country style

 cheddar with aromatic jams
p. 40

 beet and pumpkin ravioli
p. 120

 frittata with radicchio & walnut salad
p. 42

 salad with borage flowers
p. 136

 spinach and pine nut long cake
p. 162

coffee semifreddo
p. 66

#winter

 risotto with parmigiano tuiles
p. 20

 chicken teriyaki with black beans
p. 56

 moist chocolate cake
p. 74

#kids

 square pizza
p. 87

 square burger with french fries
p. 60

 cakesicles
p. 108

#summer

 gazpacho
p. 38

 pissaladière
p. 62

 mezzemaniche with broccoli and ricotta
p. 156

tarte citron
p. 30

#fall

 truffled quail eggs
p. 22

 beet and pumpkin ravioli
p. 120

 fox grape pudding
p. 126

#mediterranean

 sablé tart with anchovies
p. 140

 carrot salad with kefta
p. 46

 pomegranate and pistachio bulgur
p. 88

 fruit salad and sesame brittle
p. 48

#happy hour

 gazpacho
p. 38

 tuna tartare and guacamole
p. 98

 nigiri set
p. 100

deconstructed russian salad
p. 26

 pork loin with sesame seeds
p. 158

 pissaladière
p. 62

rye bread appetizers
p. 16

#square

 square burger with french fries
p. 60

 square pizza
p. 87

 tarte citron
p. 30

#romantic

 seared salmon with venere rice
p. 104

 sea bream tartare with rose petals
p. 106

 round meringue with wild strawberries
p. 92

#round

 lemon linguine
p. 24

 **sea bream tartare
with rose petals**
p. 106

**octopus salad
with purple puree**
p. 124

**round meringue with wild
strawberries**
p. 92

#picnic

 **spinach and pine nut
long cake**
p. 162

 **cheddar with aromatic
jams**
p. 40

 **pomegranate and pistachio
bulgur**
p. 88

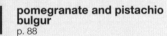 **savory asparagus tarts**
p. 160

 pissaladière
p. 62

 moist chocolate cake
p. 74

#meditation

 truffled quail eggs
p. 22

 **cream of asparagus
+ salted biscuits**
p. 155

 salad with borage flowers
p. 136

 **fruit salad and sesame
brittle**
p. 48

#sea

 **octopus salad
with purple puree**
p. 124

 **red mullet
on sweet potato**
p. 44

 sablé tart with anchovies
p. 140

 **mango pudding
with panna cotta**
p. 28

#happy
birthday

 cakesicles
p. 108

 donuts
p. 144

 brownies&whities
p. 68

 **round meringue with wild
strawberries**
p. 92

#creamy

 **deconstructed
russian salad**
p. 26

 creamed peas
p. 154

 **sea bream tartare
with rose petals**
p. 106

 tiramisù
p. 70

#elegant

 truffled quail eggs
p. 22

 **seared salmon
with venere rice**
p. 104

 **octopus salad
with purple puree**
p. 124

 coffee semifreddo
p. 66

#spicy

 rye bread appetizers
p. 16

**pomegranate and pistachio
bulgur**
p. 88

 **tandoori chicken
with basmati rice**
p. 90

 fox grape pudding
p. 126

#meatlover

 carrot salad with kefta
p. 46

 **square burger
with french fries**
p. 60

 **chicken teriyaki
with black beans**
p. 56

 **mango pudding
with panna cotta**
p. 28

#made
in italy

 square pizza
p. 87

 tiramisù
p. 70

#easy
usa

 **square burger
with french fries**
p. 60

 donuts
p. 144

#me myself
and i

 **tandoori chicken
with basmati rice**
p. 90

 **fruit salad and sesame
brittle**
p. 48

#veg

 round vegetarian burger
p. 61

 **cabbage with chickpeas
dumplings**
p. 118

 **fruit salad and sesame
brittle**
p. 48

#3shapes

 **risotto with
parmigiano tuiles**
p. 20

 **octopus salad
with purple puree**
p. 124

 blueberry cheesecake
p. 128

#lafrance

 pissaladière
p. 62

 **sea bream tartare
with rose petals**
p. 106

 tarte citron
p. 30

featured licensed products

---

pp. 25, 39, 50–51, 130–131, 152–153: Plates by
SERAX

pp. 32–33: Notebook by WW (Whitbread&Wilkinson);
Pantone "Jazzy" bookcase for iPad Air 2, easy
access to all device features while remaining design
concious. A hallmark of Case Scenario products;
Speakers by KAKKOii

pp. 64–65: Pantone "Aurora" cover. The new travel
case for iPhone 6/6s by Case Scenario

pp. 72–73: Pantone 2 metres fabric lightning cable
by Case Scenario

p. 86: Metal Box Seletti – Pantone 17-5641 –
cm 30x22 h 11 – Emerald – www.seletti.it; Vase
by SERAX

p. 101: Sticks by Room Copenhagen A/S

pp. 102–103: Sticks + Bowls + Trays by Room
Copenhagen A/S; Vases by SERAX

pp. 110–111: Bowl + Emerald Mug by Room
Copenhagen A/S

pp. 122–123: Key tray + Mug + Food container by
Room Copenhagen A/S

pp. 146–147: Placemat by WW (Whitbread&Wilkinson)

pp. 166–167: Medium Tray + Mugs by WW
(Whitbread&Wilkinson)

pp. 286–287: Notebook + Coasters + Coffee maker
+ Mugs by WW (Whitbread&Wilkinson)